How to be a successful
successful
choir
director

How to be a successful choir director

John Bertalot

Kevin Mayhew

First published in 2002 by
KEVIN MAYHEW LTD
Buxhall, Stowmarket, Suffolk, IP14 3BW
Email: info@kevinmayhewltd.com

9 8 7 6 5 4 3 2 1

ISBN 1 84003 865 9
ISMN M 57024 021 0
Catalogue Number 1450246

Front cover design by Angela Selfe
Edited by Peter Dainty
Typesetting by Richard Weaver

Printed and bound in Great Britain

Prologue

The phone rang in my home in the north of England shortly after I had returned to my homeland after sixteen most happy and fruitful years in Princeton, New Jersey, USA.

'Hello, John. It's Noel Rawsthorne from Liverpool. Welcome back to the U.K. How are you spending your retirement?'

'Oh, I'm visiting choirs for the RSCM, and adjudicating at music festivals and also leading a lot of choral workshops all over the country. What are you doing?'

'I'm enjoying learning how to paint. I've got hold of a great series of "How To" books: "How To Draw Trees", "How To Draw People", "How To Paint Landscapes". You just pick up a book, read a page, and do what it says – and it works.'

He paused for a moment and added: 'You've conducted choirs and led choral workshops all over the world; why don't you write a book full of practical suggestions which really work on "How To Be a Successful Choir Director"?'

So I did.

Dedication

To my parents, who gave me life and who supported and encouraged me in my quest to make music; and to my cousin Sheila Humphrey Charge, who took me to join my local parish church choir when I was 8 and thus started me on my career in church music.

Biographical details

Dr John Bertalot won organ scholarships to the Royal College of Music, London; Lincoln College, Oxford; and Corpus Christi College, Cambridge – where he studied respectively with Dr Harold Darke, Dr Egon Wellesz and Dr Boris Ord.

His first appointment was at St Matthew's Church, Northampton – the church for which Britten composed *Rejoice in the Lamb* – and he was the conductor of the Northampton Bach Choir and Symphony Orchestra. He also founded the St Matthew's Singers, and was visiting tutor in organ and piano at Stowe School.

He was then appointed director of music of Blackburn Cathedral which had, and still has, one of the largest wholly volunteer cathedral choirs of men and boys in England. He founded the Blackburn Bach Choir, which won the *Let the Peoples Sing* competition for two years in succession. For eighteen years he was also Senior Lecturer at the Royal Northern College of Music, Manchester, where he taught choir training, music history, composition and counterpoint.

His last full-time appointment was in Princeton, New Jersey, where for sixteen years he led one of the most ambitious Episcopal Church music programmes in the USA. He was also adjunct associate professor at Rider University. He founded the Princeton Singers, which was acclaimed as one of the finest mixed voice choirs in the USA. They also gave concerts to capacity audiences in Westminster Abbey, the Hereford Three Choirs' Festival and the Chapel of King's College, Cambridge.

During his forty years of professional music making, he led choral workshops all over the world, and his compositions are published by over a dozen publishing houses on both sides of the Atlantic.

In 1998 he retired to live in England, where his time is filled with leading choral workshops, adjudicating at music festivals and composing. He has also become organist of a village church in the middle of the Lancashire countryside, where he still puts into practice the techniques revealed in this book – and they all work!

Contents

Preface

When you give instructions to your choir you want them to listen to every word you say – but they don't. They talk instead. You're not alone. Sixty per cent of choir directors all over the world experience the same problem.

You want your choir to arrive punctually for rehearsals – but they don't. Fifty per cent of choir directors have the same problem.

You want to be able to give instructions only once – but you find that your choir doesn't really listen to you. Seventy-five per cent of choir directors also find that they have to repeat instructions.

These percentages come from surveys carried out for me by one of my publishers in the USA – and they are confirmed over and over again by the experience of choir directors who attend my workshops.

You know that your choir ought to be able to sing better than they do, but you don't have the time or the patience to do anything about it – not with the sort of singers you have. Choir directors I have met in England, the USA, Canada, South Africa, New Zealand and Australia – be they conductors of school or church or cathedral choirs, or even conductors of long-established choral societies – share many similar problems. But some directors seem to have little idea how to go about correcting or solving them or, if they do know what to do, they don't do it.

Having enjoyed, for over fifty years, the experience of conducting school and university choirs, small and large church choirs, professional and amateur choirs, and cathedral and secular choirs all over the world, especially in Great Britain and the United States, and having experienced many of these problems myself and wrestled with the necessity of solving them, I believe that choir directors would welcome some immediately practical hints which really work about how to overcome these problems. I have already written two books on choir training, which many people have found helpful, and this book offers even more practical guidance to enable choir directors to fulfil their vocation positively, courageously and fruitfully.

All improvements in your choir will involve you in extra work. If you want the members of your choir to work harder for you, you must work harder for them. If you're not prepared to spend this extra time, stop reading now. But if you *are* willing to make changes, look at the contents list in this book and mark the things which apply to your situation, so that you can begin, the more easily, to

start the process of improvement. These ideas do work –
I've tried them all. And if you try them they'll work for
you too.

John Bertalot   *Blackburn, 2002*

NB: The conductor of a choir can have many titles: director
of music, choral conductor, choir leader and so on. When
the term 'choir director' is used in this book, it covers all
these titles, and it also refers to both male and female leaders.

English names have been used for the note values:
quaver, crotchet, minim and semibreve, which are also
known as eighth, quarter, half and whole notes.

CHAPTER 1

Encourage punctuality

Facing up to the problem

Many choir directors complain that their rehearsals always start late in spite of their constant nagging reminders. Can anything be done about it? Of course it can, if you are really determined that it should. It's essential that you begin with a clear vision in your mind that you want to start punctually. Feel strongly and passionately about it; a woolly desire for punctuality is not enough. You have to be wholly passionate about everything you do in this life to stand any chance of success, be it creating a choir or creating a baby. And you need the courage to show your choir that you are the kind of person who can see things through to a successful conclusion.

Discuss the problem of unpunctuality with other interested parties: for example, your minister, if it's a church choir, or your chairperson, if it's a choral society. Let them know that you really want to tackle the problem, and enlist their moral support and practical input.

These are the steps you should take:

1. Start your rehearsals punctually

Begin your next practice on time, however few people may have arrived. Do *not* say, 'We'll wait a few minutes, because we need more singers here.' Start punctually even if you only have two sopranos and a goat.

2. Address the choir

Halfway through the practice, when everyone has finally arrived, ask them all to sit down, because you have something important to say. Wait until they're all listening before you speak. If some of them continue talking, don't keep repeating, 'Please be quiet', because waiting calmly without speaking is one of the strongest ways there is for achieving silence.

Then talk about the important place the choir occupies in the church or town. Remind them that the essence of a choir is that all voices should sing together, and that includes starting together – not just starting the music together, but starting the rehearsals together.

Ask them if there are any problems about arriving on time each week. Some may have problems with babysitters, or have to rely on public transport. Let them air their problems to get them off their chests. Listen sympathetically to what they have to say – don't interrupt. Then say, 'Yes, I understand; please have a talk with me after tonight's rehearsal.'

3. Next week

Give them all a firm goal for next week. Tell them that, from now on, you will be starting all practices exactly on time – so that all the time available can be efficiently used. Every choir member will then know that the time they spend at your rehearsals will be really worthwhile and their experience of working with you will be really rewarding. (If it isn't, you'll have to do something about that too.)

Immediate follow up

Having established the principle of the importance of punctuality, follow it up with five practical things, as follows:

1. Buy a large clock, with a second hand, and put it on a wall in your practice room so that you can see it while you're conducting. Let that clock govern the timing of your rehearsals. Using your watch as the norm for punctual starts is not good enough; it may be fast or it may be slow, and in any case your singers can't see it. Therefore there must be a standard time which everyone accepts – and that should be on a clock which everyone can see.

2. Always arrive first – at least fifteen minutes before the rehearsal is due to begin (better still, thirty minutes beforehand) to ensure that everything is ready for your singers – the chairs set out neatly and the music prepared. And so, when your singers begin to arrive, they will be welcomed by a really tidy room and won't have to spend two hours among piles of old music and last week's polystyrene coffee cups lying around in corners. They will also be welcomed by you, chatting informally with them. Never leave your preparation so late that you don't have time to talk to your singers one on one when they arrive. Why should they want to sing under your leadership if you show that you're only interested in them as singers and not as people? All choirs have an important social as well as a musical dimension. You, as their leader, should encourage both sides of this coin.

3. Make your practice really worthwhile – full of productive work and laced with good humour, so that they will say afterwards, 'My word, that was a great rehearsal. I'm glad I came.' (To do that, see for example Chapters 4, 5, 14, 15 and 23.)

4. Finish the practice absolutely on time. Thus you will be offering a complementary courtesy to them in response to their courtesy to you and to each other.

5. Always be the last to leave. Stay behind afterwards to talk informally with individual choir members. That is part of the responsibility of leadership – a leadership which requires servanthood. Unless you spend yourself for your singers, you can't expect them to spend themselves for you. If they are giving more time and effort to the choir than you are, there's something wrong.

Dealing with the latecomers

What do you do if, after you have followed this strategy, some choir members still arrive late?

First of all, it's important to **remain courteous**. When they come in late, welcome them, briefly, with a smile and a word: 'Hi, Dorothy – we're on page so-and-so.' You don't know why they're late – they may have had an accident or there may be some other good reason why they didn't arrive on time, so welcome them, however put-off you may feel. Make them feel glad to be there. If you don't make them feel welcome, they may not feel inclined to come next week. When singers occasionally arrived late for my village church choir rehearsal, we interrupted what we were singing by greeting them with broad smiles and a brief, but hearty, round of applause. That gave the message, 'Although you're late, we're very pleased you came.' They're always punctual now!

After the practice, always have a quiet, sympathetic word with the latecomer. 'Sorry you had a problem tonight – it was good to have you here.' Thus they will know that you really care about them while also caring about the matter of punctuality. They should *always* tell you why they were late. (If you have a children's choir, the child should come up to you at the piano when they arrive and whisper why they're late. This shows courtesy to the choir, and reinforces the importance of punctuality.) Always accept the reason for lateness with a smile, and never with a frown. If you don't have a quiet word afterwards with latecomers, the message they get from your silence will be that you don't really mind that they were late, so they can be late again.

Persistent latecomers

Sometimes a latecomer may not have a good reason, and this shows that they have a negative attitude about punctuality. The cultivation of punctuality is a positive virtue, not an onerous duty. It is a positive attribute rather than an oppressive obligation. People who constantly arrive late do so because they don't feel that the event to which they are coming is really important or worthwhile. They need to show that *they* are 'important', and therefore they 'make an entrance' so that everyone can feel that now they're here the rehearsal can really begin.

This is an unwritten rule for party-goers. The most important guest nearly always arrives last and leaves first. You've got to get your persistent latecomers out of this attitude of mind by showing them that they are important to you. Until they realise that, they won't feel that you are important to them.

The need to feel important arises from insecurity on their part. Really secure people don't need to show that they're important. Therefore, persistent latecomers need your help to enable them to overcome their insecurity by showing them that they are loved. Perhaps you could give them a solo to sing, or give them a job as librarian or the organiser of some regular event such as a choir party, or ask them to lead the prayers at the beginning of next week's rehearsal.

Very persistent latecomers

If there is anyone who still comes late after all this, discuss the situation with your minister or chairperson. You cannot allow this situation to continue, because it will damage the spirit of the entire choir.

Some of your choir members will test you, consciously or unconsciously, in every innovation which you introduce. They are trying to find out if you really mean it. Show them that you do by seeing it through to a successful conclusion. This will cost time and effort and firm perseverance but you'll grow in the process, and so will they.

CHAPTER 2

Begin rehearsals efficiently

Off to a good start?

I attended a choir rehearsal in a church recently where the choir director clapped his hands when the practice was due to start and said, 'Let's begin!' – but only a few of the choir members took any notice, and so he clapped his hands again. But then someone asked him a question and he went over and talked with her. In other words, he didn't really mean it when he clapped his hands for silence – and his choir knew it and responded (or rather, didn't respond) accordingly.

I suffered from this problem for many years until I suddenly realised how to solve it.

1. Mean what you say

You need to give your choir a clear sign which they will all recognise, so that they will know you are ready to begin the practice and must give you their undivided attention. The signal may be a slow *arpeggio* on the piano, or it may be the announcement of a prayer, or it may be a tap of your baton and the words: 'Good evening, ladies and gentlemen; may we begin.' (See below.) But whatever it is, show that you mean it. Wait, without speaking, until they are all quiet and ready.

2. Explain your intentions

If there has been a slow response to your signal to begin, when they are all listening, say, 'That is no way for a choir of our standard to start a rehearsal. You've all come here tonight in order to enjoy singing together, and I know that you want this to be an efficient choir and a happy choir. Therefore, next week, at 7.30' (or whenever your practice is due to begin) 'I'll play a slow *arpeggio* on the piano – taking ten seconds. During those ten seconds you'll have time to finish talking with your neighbour, and then I want you all to turn to me' (or to stand) 'and we'll begin the practice. Does anyone have a problem with that?'

3. Practise your instructions

Do *not* at that point go straight on with the rehearsal. In order to reinforce what you've just said about starting efficiently, the choir need to practise it, so that they know exactly what to do next week and the week after, and the week after that. Therefore, say to them, 'In a moment I'll ask you all to talk to your neighbour, and then, after a few moments, I'll play my slow *arpeggio*. You'll have time to finish your sentence, and then we'll all be ready to begin.' (Pause) 'Right, talk.'

Let them talk for at least half a minute – long enough to begin to run out of steam. Then play your slow *arpeggio*, and almost everyone will stop talking. I say, '*almost* everyone' because it may well be that one or two will carry on talking after the *arpeggio* has ended. They are testing you.

4. Persistent talkers

If two singers continue to talk, despite the very clear agreement reached between you and your choir, I suggest you do two things. First, look at those singers who are not talking and say with a smile, 'Thank you – that worked well.' Second, give a quick glance at the talkers and say, without a smile, 'Please see me afterwards.' These words will leave those to whom they are addressed feeling uneasy. They know that they tested you, and they also know that you passed the test.

And so, at the end of the practice, after you thanked your choir for a good rehearsal, say to those two talkers, 'May we have a quick word, please?' This will show the whole choir that you really meant what you said. When they come to you, ask them quietly, 'Was there a problem tonight, because I thought we'd all agreed that we would be ready to start after my signal.' Let them talk, briefly, but don't allow yourself to argue. Be firm, be brief, and let them leave you feeling good, not bad, about the situation. So you might end with, 'We all value your membership of the choir. I'm sure that next week we'll enjoy an even better practice. Thank you.'*

5. An alternative signal

Another sure way to begin a church choir practice efficiently is to say, 'The Lord be with you', wait for their response ('and also with you') and then say, 'Let us pray.' – and you'll get complete silence.

Always make sure, when you give an order, that you are standing up straight, like an officer in front of his troops, and looking everyone in the eye. Then speak up, speak confidently, and speak briefly: 'Good evening – may we begin.' Having given your command commandingly, lead your troops into a thoroughly rewarding rehearsal.

* I've written about a crucial moment like this in my book, *Immediately Practical Tips for Choral Directors* (published by Augsburg Fortress and available from the RSCM).

CHAPTER 3

Cure irregular attendance

If you can't rely on all your singers being there for practices or services, this is how to deal with it.

Clarify your aims

First ask yourself what you really want from your choir members. Do you really want 100 per cent attendance, or will 90 per cent do? You can confidently aim for 100 per cent – and this is the way to achieve it.

Clarify your policy

Your singers would find it helpful if, after discussion with your committee, you laid down exactly what was expected of them. Therefore, appoint an attendance officer who will present attendance records to your committee for discussion at the end of the quarter. You can aim for 100 per cent attendance if you count an excused absence as an attendance. When singers give notice that they will be absent, that is nearly as good as being there. Some Rotary Clubs allow a similar courtesy to their members. You should make allowances for family holidays, sickness and other valid reasons for absence.

If the policy of regular attendance is sent to potential new members before they join, and if this policy is reinforced occasionally in the letters of appreciation that you send to all your singers, you will have established an attendance policy which every member will tend to honour. Membership of your choir is a special privilege and not something which they can do if they have nothing better to occupy their time. It is up to you, of course, to make sure they realise that regular attendance at your rehearsals is a privilege as well as a pleasure.

As Dr Lionel Dakers said when he was director of the Royal School of Church Music, 'The only voluntary factor about joining a voluntary choir is the voluntary act of joining. After that, everything is compulsory.' Exactly! But it is essential that a policy based on this firm principle has the strong backing of your choir committee. A choir committee is like an organisational aspirin – it can be the means of curing almost every problem that will come your way. (You do have a choir committee, don't you?)

Reinforce your policy

Reinforce the committee's policy with the following practical measures:

1. Get a blackboard or large notice board and place it near the piano. On it write the names of those singers who have sent their apologies for absence that night (and the apologies of those who told you they'd be late). This is a courtesy from them to their colleagues.

2. Follow it up immediately if someone is absent and hasn't sent apologies, preferably with a phone call when you get home that night: 'Sorry you couldn't be with us this evening; we missed you. I hope everything's OK at home.'

If you don't follow up every unexplained absence immediately, you will have given permission for that singer to be absent again without telling you. (The same holds good for attendance of the committee itself. Every unexplained absence must be followed up by the chairperson or secretary, otherwise the message that the absentee receives is: 'They didn't really miss me, so next time I can't go I needn't tell them.')

Following up unexplained absences immediately gives the clear message: 'You are important to us, and your absence diminished us tonight. We all need you.' The longer you delay the follow-up, the less effect it will have. If you aren't prepared to do this, you haven't fully recognised the responsibility of being your choir's leader. If you really don't think you can do this personally, consult with your minister or committee and appoint someone who can – someone who is respected by their peers.

3. If you have a choir notice board, let there be **a sign-out sheet** on which your singers may give notice of forthcoming absences. Transfer this information onto your blackboard every week for all to see, so that your choir may know how highly you regard regularity of attendance.

The responsibility of membership

When someone joins an organisation, such as Inner Wheel, or a keep-fit class, or your choir, they need to know that that organisation is efficiently run and that they will gain benefit from their membership. And the privilege of membership implies responsibility to the other members. A choir is a close-knit team rather like a sports team; when one of the team is missing, all the members suffer. The more they give, the more they will value their membership. Aiming at high standards is the surest way to attract committed members.

If you feel that this will involve you in more work, you must realise that the extra work will lead to genuine improvement in the life of your choir – that is what this book is all about. Every improvement will make your extra effort worthwhile, so be courageous – try it.

CHAPTER 4
Raise musical standards

Aim for the highest

Are you content to accept that the members of your choir are doing their little best in their own little way, and that high standards are not really appropriate in your situation? Does your choir like things to stay as they are, or wistfully remark that things were much better in the good old days – 'looking forward to the past' as the playwright John Osborne once said?

Many choirs do not reach the high standards of which they are capable – because their director (i) isn't aware of what high standards are, (ii) wouldn't believe that their choir could reach them, even if they did know, and (iii) doesn't know how to go about reaching those high standards.

Because you are reading this, let's take it for granted that there are such things as high standards to aim for. Your choir can reach higher standards, and they will enjoy the experience, even with the miscellaneously gifted, or ungifted, singers you have right now. Try to start believing this. Don't go on to the next stage until you feel passionately that you want your choir to sing better.

Make a start

Set high standards during the first few seconds of the rehearsal. This gives the message to the choir that they must give of their very best. It's the equivalent of drill in the army – they have to 'snap to attention' several times before they are *able* to feel that they are a team. You are enabling them to sing well – that's what they've come there for. So, the standard you reach in the first few seconds will be the standard you achieve for the rest of the practice. You won't be able to get any better standard afterwards, because you will have shown them what your standards are in those first few vital moments.

Practical ideas

1. The choir is a team and you are its coach. Do everything on that basis. The essence of a good choir is that all its members pull together, that they are clearly focused on what they are aiming for, and that the conductor knows more about choral music than the members and has the skill and technique to help them raise their standards.

'Pulling together' involves, initially, the co-operative spirit behind punctuality and regular attendance. We've dealt with this. You've got to get that right first.

2. Realise that singers want to sing well, not badly. Many choirs are not clearly focused (e.g. they don't sing together, don't sing in tune, don't make a beautiful sound, don't blend) because their conductors don't lead their practices to achieve all these things. They put up with untidy attacks and wrong notes and lazy stance and no expression, because they don't want to find fault with the nice people who live in the parish and who are kind enough to sing in their choir.

3. Correct your singers' faults. I know several choir directors who think, subconsciously, that correcting a singer's wrong notes is actually finding fault with the singer as a person – it's bad manners. They think it's as impolite as going into your friend's house and saying that it's untidy. But no singer joins a choir to sing wrong notes on purpose. They only sing wrong notes because they don't know how to sing right ones. And the only person who can show them how to sing right ones is the conductor – and that's you.

If your choristers are singing wrong notes and know that they are, and if you don't do anything to correct them, the message will come through, 'The conductor doesn't care about right notes', or 'The director can't hear when we sing incorrectly.' Either message means that the singers needn't try so hard, and you'll find it difficult to achieve anything really worthwhile.

Of course, there are some choir directors who don't correct wrong notes, because they don't hear them. This is how to deal with that problem if you suffer from it.

(a) Do your homework. Before you can dare to teach your choir how to sing an anthem correctly you have to learn the music yourself beforehand. If you are a director who faithfully prepares all the music beforehand – even the easy music – marking awkward places where singers could go wrong, and where breaths should be taken, give yourself a hearty pat on the back. You are, literally, one in a hundred.

(b) Be precisely concise. Some choir directors talk too much. (*All* choir directors talk too much!) We theorise for a boring minute about the music, instead of honing in on exactly what it is that we want our choir to do: 'I want you to sing this page with great sincerity, with a feeling of

breadth, with long sweeping lines and making a lovely sound. Think about the historical context in which this lovely music was written. Think about the theological implications of blah, blah, blah.' By that time all the singers have turned off, and nobody will be listening to you.

Say instead, 'Sing the first four bars in one breath – most of you are breathing after the second bar. Don't.' They'll sing it again for you, but some singers will still breathe after the second bar – either because they're testing you (to see if you really mean it) or, more likely, because they're not thinking. So, after the second attempt, say, 'Some of you are still breathing after the second bar. Don't.' Get them to do it again. Demonstrate what you want (making sure, when demonstrating, that you sing the passage well – some choir directors don't, or can't). But there'll still be at least one singer who is singing it in-correctly. So your choir will have to sing it one more time. 'Well done. Now go back to the bottom of the previous page and we'll sing it in context.'

(c) *Stay with it till they get it right.* Show them that you mean what you say. If they sing it correctly in context, look surprised and smile. If they don't, decide whether or not you really meant all of them to get it right or just most of them. If you only want most of them to be right, they'll know, and their standards will immediately begin to slip. 'Our conductor didn't really mean it, so we needn't try so hard.'

Many choir directors, when they define a fault, ask their singers to sing the passage again and then they let it go without any comment, or, worse still, they say, 'Good', when it's not good.

Many choirmasters automatically say, 'Good', after their choir has tried to correct a passage. I've told my village church choir that when I say, 'Good', I really mean, 'Bad!' (though said with a smile). Recently, when I said, 'Quite remarkable,' one bass commented, 'You mean that was really awful, don't you?'. So watch out for these automatic responses which come to us so easily – or tell your choir what your 'Good' *really* means!

Because you ask your choir to sing a passage again cor-rectly doesn't mean that they will get it right. They sang it wrong because they didn't know how to sing it right. You told them how to sing it accurately, but they need to prac-tise the experience of getting it right, which means singing it at least twice more to ensure that everyone gets it right.

It's the same with practising the piano; once you work out how to play a passage correctly you know that you will need to play it right at least three times before your fingers feel easy about playing it correctly. Choirs need to be rehearsed in the same way. Your singers need to sing a passage correctly at least twice before it's secure for Sunday – better still, get them to sing it three times correctly – but raise the standard by challenging them to sing it a little better each time: 'Was that really soft?'; 'Did you all sing the "d" on "and" in bar three?'; 'Did we start absolutely together?' Present only one of these challenges at a time, for each repeated attempt. Singers can't remember more than one thing at a time. Therefore focus your rehearsals on getting one point securely right before you move on to the next one.

Not many of us are called to do the extraordinary – to direct the music of a great cathedral or nationally famous choir. But all of us who lead music in our schools or churches or local choral societies are called to do the ordinary extraordinarily well. And that's what this book is all about.

CHAPTER 5

Make demands on your choir

Don't nanny your choir

Some conductors give their choir too much unnecessary help, for example by always playing the piano with them or singing along to encourage them. They don't need that sort of help. If you nanny them like that, they'll stay babies. They need stretching – and that means making demands on them.

1. Don't play over well-known tunes

Too many choir directors play a hymn tune all the way through before they ask their choir to sing it. Some directors of cathedral choirs even play the psalm chant through before they ask their choirs to sing the psalm. The act of playing through a well-known tune, even the first two lines, is a sure way to turn off your singers' concentration; and the essence of achieving clearly focused singing from your choir is to enable and encourage every singer to concentrate for the whole of your rehearsal.

Surely your choir can sing 'Praise, my soul' or 'Onward Christian soldiers' without you having to play the first two lines through? You may think that you're helping them when you do this, or giving them sufficient time to find the place. But all you're doing is saying, in effect, 'The next twenty seconds are turn-off time; you needn't listen to what I'm playing.' And once you give that message to them – that they needn't really listen to what you're playing – they won't. That's why some of them will start talking, because you're wasting their time.

(By the way, if you can show your choir how to sing psalm chants and hymn tunes musically, you will be an exceptional choir director. Many choirs sing through their chants as though they were chewing prunes – in other words, just to get the notes right. But if you can encourage your choir to make little *crescendos* and *diminuendos* in each 'quarter' of the chant while they sing a continuous 'Ah', they will find that they will be able to sing the psalm so much more musically. The same applies to hymn tunes and also to the singing of warm-ups.)

2. Keep accompaniment to a minimum

If you have to accompany your choir on the piano because they're not quite sure of the tune or harmony, try playing with detached chords. Instead of playing legato crotchets, try playing the tune in a succession of quaver chords with quaver rests (i.e. very staccato crotchets). Then the choir will be able to hear themselves, instead of fighting against the continuous piano sounds – and, what's more, you will be able to hear the choir.

Silence enhances concentration. So try this. Announce the number of the hymn firmly (whatever you say to a choir, let it always be said firmly, otherwise they won't listen) and wait for ten seconds in silence. (This ten seconds will sharpen their concentration, and that's exactly what you are aiming for.) Then play the first chord once – firmly – look at them expectantly for three more seconds, catching everyone's eye in a sweeping glance to make contact with them all, and then bring them in for the first verse without playing the piano again. Let them sing unaccompanied.

I visited a fine church choir recently, where the young choir director played every tune through on the piano before he asked the choir to sing. Then he accompanied their singing with very firm playing, and he had to concentrate so hard on playing the right notes that he couldn't listen to the choir. I stood this for two minutes before I asked him if I could take over. I asked the choir to begin the first verse again, in unison, without accompaniment, and without another note being given. They immediately perked up, because they had to sing on their own – and they sang superbly.

Their director whispered to me a minute later that he'd never thought of asking his choir to sing without the piano. He realised that he could actually hear what they were doing when they sang by themselves. And so I asked him to lead the next hymn. He gave the first chord, and then began accompanying the choir yet again. I sidled up to him and asked, *sotto voce*, 'Why are you playing?' 'It's become a habit,' he said contritely, and he stopped playing. The choir sang on, and they sang far better because the responsibility for singing that hymn had been given to them.

3. Give your choir responsibility

That is the essence of training a choir. They will respond if you give them high standards to aim for and the responsibility to lead. Many choir directors don't do that, and that's why their choirs don't lead the singing and speaking of their congregations.

Does the singing of your choir make your congregation sit up and want to join in enthusiastically? Does the way that your choir sings those eternal truths suddenly reveal to the people in the pews a truth that they hadn't realised before?

In order to make that happen, you first have to understand and rejoice in those truths yourself and communicate them to your choir. 'Thou art the Way, by THEE alone . . .'.

Hymns encapsulate the theology of the people, because in hymns our understanding about God and the Gospel is put into simple, straightforward terms which everyone can understand immediately. 'There is a green hill . . . where the dear Lord was CRUCIFIED, who DIED to SAVE us all.' 'Come, thou long-expected Jesus, born to set thy people FREE . . .'. Your choir is there to lead the congregation, not only in singing enthusiastically, but also in understanding the words they are singing. Therefore, if you're to do your job as a church choral director effectively, you need to appreciate some essential Christian theology.

4. Challenge your singers

The essence of good practices is continually to challenge your singers to sing better than they think they can. Introduce each new challenge one at a time, believing in your heart of hearts that they will be able to achieve what you have asked of them.

(a) Get their attention

At the beginning of a practice you have before you a collection of individuals. It's your job, within the first ten seconds of the practice, to weld them together into a choir – and a choir is a body of singers which feels a corporate sense of identity. That implies a strong sense of self-discipline – which means listening to every word that their director says. So make sure that everything you say is worth listening to.

Many choir directors start with warm-ups. These can be a very useful way of starting rehearsals, for the singers know that they can do them well. A practice that begins well will almost certainly continue to go well.

Other choir directors get their choir to sing the first chord of a well-known hymn tune absolutely together – hummed (to help produce easy forward tone) or sung to a vowel ('Ee' or 'Ah' or 'Oo'). When singing 'Ee' make sure your singers sing with their lips pushed forward, not stretched wide. Try it for yourself before you ask them to do it, so that you may experience for yourself which sounds better.

The beginning of a rehearsal is like the drilling of troops by a sergeant (a kind-hearted one). He calls them to attention, and immediately they change from being a collection of individuals into a disciplined body. So the conductor, with an encouraging, firm and good-humoured approach, should immediately transform the choir into a self-disciplined team. This sets a high standard right from the start.

An effective way to do this is to ask your singers to stand up together, watching the leaders on either side of the choir (see 'Standing and sitting', page 120). This will immediately bring them 'to attention'.

(b) Go on to ever higher standards

Like a good drill sergeant, however, the perceptive conductor will not be satisfied with just one call to 'attention' (when the choir attempts to sing the first chord absolutely together, or when they sing their warm-ups), but will encourage them to raise their standards by getting them to sing better and better – 'Did you all breathe together with me?' 'Did you all drop your jaws to sing "Ah"?' 'Are you all standing really well?' 'Is everyone's diaphragm working as it should?'

Never be satisfied with what your choir sings because, once you are satisfied with what they've just sung, you are in effect telling them, 'You can never sing that any better.' And so your striving for higher standards will come to an abrupt halt.

Let me stress this point: whenever you ask your choir to sing an anthem which they've been rehearsing, by all means say, 'Well done!', and then add, 'But . . .' Never just 'run through' an anthem, but always find at least one thing that they can polish that little bit more, even if it's singing just the last chord really together, or checking the rhythm of a few bars elsewhere. Once you've shown that you think they could never sing that anthem any better, they never will. Asking them to sing one small passage again to improve unanimity or intonation will spur your singers to try even harder for you. And that's what you want from them, and what they want from you.

(c) Higher standards for everyone

You may object that if a choir is made up of sensitive older people who can't really sing well, they shouldn't be subjected to the perpetual challenge of higher and higher standards. Nevertheless, your aim for these singers should be the same as it is for more gifted singers:

1. They should enjoy every moment of your rehearsal.

2. They will enjoy working with you if you consciously enjoy working with them. (You have to give the lead in this; it's amazing how infectious joy can be.)

3. Everyone will enjoy singing a little better tonight than they sang last week.

It's up to you to decide how they can achieve this. With less gifted singers aim at getting them, for example, to sing a line of a hymn in one breath instead of two breaths. Rejoice with them when they do that. Then ask if they think they can do the same in another hymn. With more ambitious singers, help them to aim for wholly accurate notes and intonation, lovely sound, correct breathing, clear diction, and so on . . . The point is that every choir should aim for higher standards, but the standard they aim at depends on where they are right now. The achievements of your choir are restricted, not so much by the ability of the singers as by the ability and vision of the choir director.

One hundred per cent

If the standard you set for your choir is 'that's nearly right', then 'nearly' will be what you'll always get from them. They will nearly be punctual. They will nearly be regular in attendance. They will nearly make a nice sound. They will nearly listen to what you say.

'Nearly' is not good enough. If you expect 90 per cent accuracy from your twenty singers, that means that two singers will always be singing wrong notes. It sounds foolish to put it that way, but that's how it is. Your aim must be 100 per cent in everything. That doesn't necessarily mean that you're trying to make your choir sound like King's, Cambridge. It means that you'll aim to enable your choir to sing as well as they possibly can this week, which will encourage them, and you, to do even better next week. Punctuality, right notes and singing together should be your three top priorities.

CHAPTER 6

Conduct more creatively

The conductor should be in control

If you find it difficult to get your choir to follow your conducting, so that they always come in late and you sometimes have to conduct half a beat ahead of the music, there are six possible reasons for this:

1. You don't really expect your choir to come in with your beat

If you don't believe in your heart of hearts that they will come in with your beat, they won't. You hope that they will, but that's no good. You have to *know* that they will. The way to achieve this is actually to rehearse them coming in together with your beat on that first note. (See item 4 below.)

2. You don't really look at them

You may think that you look at your choir when you bring them in, but in fact you probably drop your eyes to your copy of the music at the crucial moment. Ninety-five per cent of choral conductors do this. I was talking to a conductor recently and she agreed that many of her colleagues had this fault – implying that she herself always looked at her singers when she brought them in. But I know that she doesn't – she nearly always drops her eyes to look at the copy. She even conducts 'Amens' while dropping her eyes to the music.

You may share this fault without knowing it. The only way to find out if you do or don't is to conduct your choir *without the music* in front of you. Surely you can conduct *Jesu, joy of man's desiring* or a similar anthem without having the music in front of you? You'll feel musically naked standing there without the comfort – the Linus-blanket comfort – of the copy before you, and you may insist that you have to look at your music every few bars. But not if you've done your homework. You should always know your music better than those to whom you are teaching it.

So learn to conduct from memory. If you don't mark your music, I suggest that you do. Mark the copy, sparingly, so that you can see, at a glance, what is happening during the next half page. For example, write a large 'P', meaning: 'There's a soft passage coming up in four bars' time', or mark the important bass entry for which they need your help. If you mark your copy in coloured pencil, you'll then be able to *refer* to your music with a quick glance, without having to put your head down to *read* it.

It's so reassuring to look at your music instead of looking at the choir, for you can then imagine what the music should sound like. But that doesn't help the singers at all – you are in fact conducting yourself and not your singers. They know that, but you don't. When you look at your music, you immediately lose contact with your choristers who carry on singing, quite happily, without you. I know of several cathedral directors of music who habitually drop their eyes to the music at crucial moments but, of course, I daren't tell them!

Make lively visual contact. You have to look your singers full in the face, and you could find this really challenging. But it's the only effective way to conduct. You'll find that, by looking at your singers all the time, you will experience real communication with them, perhaps for the first time, and they'll immediately sing far better for you.

I saw Sir Simon Rattle conduct Beethoven's Ninth Symphony recently; he conducted the entire work from memory and it was stunning. He looked his players, his choir and his soloists full in the face for the whole work, and they responded to each twitch of his eyebrow, to each expressive movement of his musical hands and to his eloquent body language. And he did it; not to show how clever he was, but to create a more worthwhile performance. If he could conduct this major work without the comfort of the music before him, surely you could try to conduct a simple song or setting of the Responses from memory – not in order to show how clever *you* are, but to get a better performance from your singers. Will you dare to try it at your next rehearsal and then at a service?

3. You're not breathing for your singers

In order to be able to begin together, singers should breathe with an open mouth exactly one beat beforehand. (Some singers breathe an approximate *half* beat before they come in – that's why first chords can be untidy.) But the conductor has to give them the lead by breathing with them. If you aren't in the habit of doing this, or if you've never tried, see if it works. It will.

But you'll have to train yourself to do it every time. I sometimes used to forget this when I was conducting my choirs in the USA, and when I asked them, 'Why didn't you come in together?' they said, 'Because you didn't breathe for us with an open mouth.' Whoops! We need to realise that good breathing is the positive power in all singing and that the taking of a breath by the conductor, exactly one beat before the choir comes in, sets this process in motion. Too many conductors conduct with their mouths firmly shut; this gives no help to their choirs at all.

By the way, show your singers that, when they take this preliminary breath, their mouths should be in the shape of the first vowel of the first word. For example: 'aw' for 'Lord', 'eh' for 'set', and 'ah' for 'my' (and explain what a diphthong is). This will prepare them to come in even more musically.

4. You haven't rehearsed your singers in following your beat

It's not enough just to say to your choir, 'Look at me'. That's just theory. What is needed is practice. Too many of us tend to say to our singers, when we are pressed for time, 'Get that right on Sunday.' No – rehearsals must be wholly practical, not theoretical. You have to say, 'Let's practise coming in on that first note.' And then you rehearse them singing that one note with your beat three times or more before you're satisfied.

And then, once they are looking at you (and you are looking at them), say, 'We'll sing those first eight bars – watch my left hand, and I'll show you whether I want you to *crescendo* or *diminuendo*.' In other words, you are saying, 'When I give you this or that sign, I expect you to respond immediately.' And so they have to be rehearsed in responding to you. It's no good just *telling* them to respond and expect them to do it, for they won't. They have to be *rehearsed* in their response to you.

Even some professional conductors I have watched don't always do this. I've seen some of the finest choral conductors in the world guest-conduct a professional choir in the USA, and when that choir didn't respond to their beat as they had hoped, they began to conduct more vigorously and even to conduct before the beat. They didn't realise that the choir was not used to their guest conductor. And so they needed to be rehearsed to respond to his beat and his signals, in the same way that wrong notes have to be corrected by practising the right ones. Think about it – especially if you are a professional conductor.

After you have rehearsed your choir several times in singing expressively in response to your clear gestures, tell them that they're going to sing the same passage again, but this time you'll speed up or slow down. Don't conduct them as if they're a herd of recalcitrant donkeys, as some conductors of children's choirs seem to do – 'They'll only respond to me if I conduct very energetic- ally' – but conduct them in the sure knowledge that they will respond to your every gesture. When they don't (and they won't first time, for they've never paid much atten- tion to you) you should stop them and ask, 'Are you get- ting louder/faster/slower? Are you singing with my beat, or after it?' When they tell you that they aren't, say, 'Well, do it!' and lead them again, using the same gestures – radiating confidence. And it still won't be wholly right, so you have to do it a third time.

If you make the mistake of conducting more energetic- ally because they aren't responding as you would wish, they will know that you have lost the argument and that *you* will have to make more effort, not they. The essence of effective conducting is so to inspire your singers that they will sing their very best – and for this they need strong, firm, clear, confident leadership from a conductor who has rehearsed them in responding to every gesture. There's no need to throw yourself about when conducting. Some of the most effective conductors I have seen use minimal ges- tures because they have rehearsed their choirs to respond to those gestures. The singers have to make the extra effort, not you.

A former conductor of King's College Choir, Cambridge, Dr Boris Ord, with whom I studied in the 1950s, used to conduct his choir by resting his hands on the music desk alongside his boys, and beating time with one finger of each hand – looking at the senior bass on the other side of the choir, who was looking at him and conducting in the same way. The concentration of those two conductors and all their singers was electric. The choir had to concentrate because the conductors used such small gestures and because the self-discipline of the whole choir was so strong.

I need to mention that Dr Ord, and his successor, Sir David Willcocks, only conducted anthems. They didn't conduct 'bread and butter' music – psalms, hymns and well-known responses. They gave responsibility for the singing of this music entirely to the choir, led by an under- graduate beater on either side, so that they would sing better, and so that they would pay more attention to them when they did conduct. I have done the same with all my choirs – and it works.

I attended a Choral Evensong in a college chapel some years ago where the director conducted the Introit, which went well, but then he stood back and let the beaters conduct the responses. As soon as he did that, the level of concentration of the whole choir rose, because the responsibility for singing had been given to them. And, of course, they sang much better.

I shall get into trouble for saying this, but I wonder why so many choir directors, especially of cathedral choirs, conduct absolutely everything – not only responses (which the singers know like the backs of their hands) but also hymns.

I visited another college chapel and attended a superb Choral Evensong where the director of music conducted everything, even the hymns. Not only was he oblivious to the fact that the choir wasn't following him but following the organ, but he also didn't realise that he sometimes sang the first note of verses all by himself, because the organ didn't come in with his beat! I was amazed, for he is a highly respected professional musician.

If your choir can't sing hymns without you conducting them, then you must have a pretty poor opinion of your singers. Conductors who do that don't realise that the choir is not following them, but following the organ.

But, in that case, you might claim that the director is conducting the organist. I would say that if the organist can't play hymns without you conducting them, then take over the organ bench yourself! Am I suggesting that some choral directors stand in front of their choirs during services because they, the directors, have to be seen to be doing something to occupy their time, while their capable assistant plays the organ? No comment!

5. You aren't relaxed enough

To get the best results from choirs, the conductor must be wholly relaxed, and yet intently focused. This is especially true for choir conductors. When a choir sees that its conductor is tense or stiff, the singers automatically become tense and stiff, and their tone suffers accordingly. If the conductor frowns, they frown. A conductor should have a relaxed wrist – similar to a pianist's or violinist's wrist. No pianist could play freely with a stiff wrist, yet many conductors, even some professional ones, conduct with stiff, taut hand movements. No wonder that their choirs respond stiffly. However, if they are a professional choir, they will still sing well despite their conductor's inadequate gestures.

I try to conduct with what I call a *harpsichord touch* – small, very precise gestures which mean a lot, and which

I know will be responded to by every singer, because I actually rehearse them in responding to my gestures before I rehearse an anthem. I and they can feel, almost physically, that my hand and facial movements are connecting with them directly. I get the mechanism right between me and the singers (like ensuring that the mechanism of a harpsichord is 100 per cent before I play it) and then I know that every gesture I make will receive an instant and sensitive response from every singer. Once the choir have grasped the meaning of their conductor's gestures and are responding fully, the need for all unnecessary gestures will disappear.

Try these practical tips:

(a) Use small gestures. The bigger the gestures when conducting, the less the singers will have to look at you, and the less, therefore, will be their response.

(b) Conduct with independent hands. Conduct the time with your right hand, and the expresssion with your left. Some choir directors conduct as though they are stirring two Christmas puddings in contrary motion. When one hand is conducting the time, there's no need for the other hand to be a mirror image. Let your left hand be used sparingly and meaningfully for expression, or phrasing, or bringing in a voice part. Mark your copy so that you can always indicate to the voice-parts in polyphonic music when they should come in. Look at them fully one bar beforehand, and then indicate, by pointing to the singers with your left hand – while your right hand is still beating time – exactly one beat before they should sing: '*and* in!'

Practice makes perfect. If you don't practise this skill, your choir will still come in late, and you'll find that you get very healthy by indulging in unnecessary exercise when standing in front of your choir. Of course you may have to conduct more vigorously when the music gets louder, but, instead of just flailing the air, it is better to let your gestures be even more 'alive' than usual.

(c) Conduct with your eyes. The most expressive part of your body when conducting is not your hands but your eyes. Dr Ord's eyes were flashing and hypnotic when he conducted. You could feel the music vibrate through his whole body – but it was his eyes which communicated his intentions to his singers.

It's possible to conduct a choir with your eyes only. Try it. Warn them what it is that you are about to do, then look at them all for a few seconds, breathe exactly one beat before they are due to come in, and then bring them in firmly with your eyes and a slight nod of the head. If you have any doubt, the choir won't respond. It's a bit like St Peter walking on the water – once he began to doubt, he started to sink. You've got to believe that they will come in with you and, with a little rehearsal, they will. And they'll be excited at what they've just achieved, and so will you.

(d) Mouth the words. One very obvious attribute that creative choir conductors have is to mouth the words that the choir is singing. This is good because it encourages the choir to sing with even more clarity of diction, and because the best conductors conduct not so much with their hands as with the expression on their faces. When conductors mouth the words with their singers they are able to animate the meaning of those words as well as to get them sung more accurately.

6. You haven't done your homework

It's essential that you rehearse conducting your music. If you have to practise a piece on the piano to make sure of a good performance, surely you need to practise conducting that choral work, however simple it may be – to make sure that every gesture is helpful to your singers.

Look at yourself in the mirror when you practise conducting, and ask yourself if your gestures would be helpful to your singers, or would they get in their way? A conductor is an enabler – it is the singers who create the sound – so let your gestures encourage (not browbeat) them to do their best.

And you need to be able to give of your best when you conduct concerts. Sir Malcolm Sargent, one of the twentieth century's leading conductors, always went to bed for two hours in the afternoon before he conducted a major concert. If he, a highly experienced and professional musician, needed to rest before major musical occasions, how much more do we, so that we may be physically and mentally prepared to inspire our singers.

CHAPTER 7

Train your choir to listen to you

The problem

Seventy-five per cent of choir directors all over the world have to tell their choirs two or three times what they want them to do before they take any notice.

If you suffer from this problem, the reason is that your choir has trained you to repeat your instructions. You think you are training your choir, but, in this matter, your choir has trained you – first, because you may not have done anything about it; and second, because much of what you say to them may not be worth listening to.

The solution

The solution is simple – but its practical application is hard.

1. Speak with conviction

You have to train yourself to speak firmly with an officer-like command, albeit good humoured and encouraging, and your instructions must be very clear and wholly practical. That's a major challenge.

Instead of saying, 'We didn't really give the feeling of confidence at the beginning of this anthem; we need to think more positively about how we're going to come in,' say with an encouraging smile, 'The first chord of this anthem was untidy. Come in exactly with my beat.' (And you will look at them encouragingly, wait three seconds, breathe for them, and then bring them in. But you will not be satisfied.) 'That's better,' you'll say, 'but the basses are still late. Basses – sing that first note with me, absolutely together.'

Always give your instructions clearly and with as few words as possible. 'Was that really soft? Let's do it again.' Many choir directors chatter needlessly before asking their choir to 'sing it again': 'I don't think that this lovely music was really as soft as it might be. I've heard choirs sing it much more quietly. I wonder if we could try it a fraction more *piano*, please. Let's start at the top of the page; here's your chord. Now, is everyone really ready to try to sing it more softly this time? Ready? Watch me!'

That's boring. No wonder your choir loses attention! But once they realise that you will give brief and clear instructions only once, the improvement in their attention level will be immediately obvious, and so the level of their singing will rise, and they will enjoy singing more; for no one wants to be a member of a disorderly team.

You must speak encouragingly, of course, but you must give your instructions audibly and firmly and look your singers straight in the face, especially singers in the back rows who sit furthest from you and who, therefore, may be inclined to pay less attention to you than those in the front rows. Don't have your head buried in your own copy of the music. A mark of officers is that they stand up straight and look at those whom they are commanding – looking them right in the eye. This is a sure way to make real contact.

2. Singers must listen, not just hear

I have found, to my great surprise, that many choristers, even in good choirs, don't really listen to their conductors. I was guest conductor of a famous choir in the USA recently and found that, at the beginning of the practice, only half of the singers did what I asked them to do – because they were used to their distinguished conductor telling them everything two or three times.

So I said, firmly but kindly, 'Ladies and gentlemen, we have a lot to rehearse tonight and it would save us valuable time if I could give my instructions only once.' They immediately came to 'attention', and the rest of the rehearsal was superb – because they raised their level of listening.

And so, when you announce the number of the hymn you're going to rehearse, and someone asks, 'What number did you say?' – don't repeat the number. Turn to one of his neighbours and say with a smile, 'Tell him what number I said.' That will make them realise that you mean what you say.

CHAPTER 8

Teach them how to breathe

Shallow breathing

Don't assume that it's natural for your singers to know how to breathe. It isn't. If there's one fault above all others that most choirs share (apart from not blending, not singing together, having no sense of rhythm and not watching the conductor) it is shallow breathing.

Most choirs breathe twice too often. This is a law. Look at these examples:

'When other helpers (breath) fail, and comforts flee'

'And did the coun- (breath) -tenance divine (breath – OK) shine forth upon (breath) those clouded hills?'

'When I survey (breath) the wondrous cross'

'In fields where they (breath) lay, keeping their sheep'

'Be still and know (breath) that I am God'

'Morning has broken (breath) like the first morning'

And, of course, there is the classic couplet where misplaced breathing completely alters the meaning of the text:

'My God, I love thee, not (breath) because
I hope for heaven thereby'

Correct breathing is also essential for lesson readers. Some seem to infer that Mary *and* Joseph *and* the babe were lying in the manger together. But a breath taken at the right place gives the correct meaning: '. . . and found Mary, and Joseph, (breath) and the babe lying in a manger.' (Luke 2:16). Similarly, clear diction is especially important when reading the Old Testament lesson about God's promises to faithful Abraham (Genesis 22:17): '. . . I will multiply thy seed as the stars of heaven, and as the sandwiches on the seashore . . .'!

Intelligent breathing

Intelligently placed breathing can also transform your choir's singing and give it new life. For example, instead of singing (at the end of 'Ev'n so in Christ' – *Messiah*):

'. . . ev'n so in Christ (breath)
shall all, shall all be made alive',

notice where the comma is (and where it isn't) and sing:

ev'n so in Christ shall all, SHALL ALL be made a - live.

The words should always make sense when you're singing. It's the matter of 'making sense' which primarily determines where your singers should, and should not, breathe. Look at Stanford's *Magnificat* in B flat. If the music were to determine where breaths should be taken, it could be phrased like this:

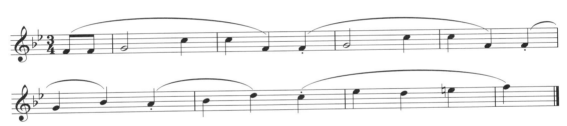

But as it's the words which inspired the music, the breathing could be amended to this:

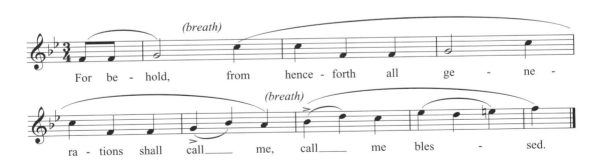

For be - hold, from hence - forth all ge - ne -
ra - tions shall call me, call me bles - sed.

It's the words that inspired the composer to create the music, so let the words inspire you too. Consider this from Mozart's *Ave Verum* –

Many choirs sing:

'Ave, ave (breath) verum corpus',

instead of (noticing the comma again):

But a word of caution: sometimes there are a lot of commas in the text. If the choir were to breathe at all those commas, the musical line would become very jagged. One needs to exercise common sense in these cases. It's sometimes helpful to ignore a few commas in order to create a more interesting musical line with phrases of different lengths. One example is the 'alleluia' chorus at the end of each verse of *Praise, my soul, the King of Heaven*. Singing two 'alleluias' in one breath, especially if you make a crescendo at the end of the first to lead on to the second, can give a musical lift to those words.

Similarly, it's sometimes good to break up the monotonous repetition of two- or four-bar phrases. In the last verse of my arrangement of *Amazing Grace** the phrase 'Praise God' is sung seven times in a row.

Some choirs sing these short phrases with a breath after every comma. I've found that this passage comes much more alive when half the commas are ignored to make longer phrases.

Good breathing is essential for good singing

Good breathing is essential if your choir is to sing musically. Think of the organ. Its pipework and its action may be first class, but if there's not a sure and steady wind supply, with plenty to spare, the whole instrument sounds bad. It's the same with choirs. The essence of good singing is to sing long phrases in one breath – and these are generally four bars long. Most singers breathe every two bars.

* Published by Augsburg Fortress

This is because they've not been challenged to think while they're singing. It's so very easy to turn off one's mind when singing a hymn. I've found that to be true of myself when I'm sitting in the congregation – my brain goes onto automatic pilot far too easily, so that I've no idea what I've been singing about for the last few minutes. This is true also for many singers in school, church and secular choirs. Ask your choir what the words mean of the song they are rehearsing. You may be surprised when you are met by an embarrassed silence.

There are three reasons why choirs breathe inadequately:

1. Their conductors don't breathe. Some conductors don't know how to breathe correctly. Ask any singer to take a quick, deep breath, and very often you'll see their shoulders rise and their diaphragms go in. This is the exact opposite of what it should be. Many conductors don't know this.

2. Their conductors don't teach. Even when conductors do know how singers should breathe, some don't realise the primary importance of teaching their singers how to do it.

3. Their conductors don't insist. Even when they do teach their choristers how to breathe correctly, especially during their warm-ups, they don't always put creative breathing into practice when rehearsing music, and so their singers don't do it.

This is how a singer should breathe:

1. Breathe horizontally. Lie flat on your back on the floor. Put your hands on your tummy and breathe naturally. You'll find that your tummy seems to fill up with air when you breathe in, and goes down when you breathe out. (Of course, it's not your tummy, it's your diaphragm we're talking about.) Do that several times so that you can feel how easy it is. It's almost impossible to breathe incorrectly when lying flat.

2. Breathe vertically. Now try to breathe in the same way when you're standing up. This may not be so easy, and many folk do the exact opposite – they pull in their tummy (diaphragm) when they breathe in, and let it go out when they breathe out. They try to fill their lungs with air, and so they raise their shoulders. This, apart from being inefficient, is uncomfortable. You can't sing easily if your shoulders are raised.

3. Breathe low. If you fill up low down with air and also keep your shoulders down and relaxed, as you did when you lay on the floor, you can take in much more air. The most accomplished singers can feel their side ribs expanding too when they breathe in. So it's a good thing for a singer, when practising breathing, to put one hand lightly on the tummy and the other hand on the side – to feel expansion when breathing in, and contraction when breathing out.

Apply good breathing to all singing

In your rehearsals, don't just practise intelligent breathing during your warming up exercises, but continually draw the attention of your choir to specific passages where they need to sing four or more bars in one breath. They do need constant reminders, otherwise they won't do it.

If they often seem to forget the places where good breathing is especially important, don't just tell them – get them to tell you. Ask them where they need to take special note of breathing in the piece of music they're rehearsing, and then, because they have to think for themselves, they'll be more likely to do it correctly thereafter.

When you conduct your anthem, all you need to do is to indicate, very gently, where they should, or should not, breathe. Conducting is all about giving firm, clear reminders, because you know, and they know, that they can do it. If they don't think they can do it, and if you doubt they can do it, well, you'll be right – they won't be able to, because you clearly show that you don't think they can. Conducting is all about radiating confidence – your confidence in your singers, which boosts their confidence in themselves.*

*For some more useful breathing exercises see my book, *Immediately Practical Tips for Choral Directors* – available from the RSCM.

CHAPTER 9

Singing as well on Sunday as at rehearsal

Choirs forget

It often happens that a choir will sing well during practice, and apply all that you have told them, but when Sunday comes they forget. They don't sing four bars in one breath, they don't take any notice of dynamics, and they don't watch their conductor.

Showing you what to do about this is, perhaps, one of the most important techniques I can share with you.

Train your choir to think for themselves

If you don't do this, they will sing automatically without thinking, because that's what you've conditioned them to do in your rehearsal.

Don't nanny them

Many choir directors are assiduous in correcting faults, in encouraging their singers to raise their standards and enabling them to enjoy rehearsals. But they treat them as though they had kindergarten mentalities; and this can apply to adult choirs as well as to children's choirs. The more you treat your singers as intelligent beings, the more intelligently and eagerly they will respond.

When choir directors point out every fault to their singers – when they nanny them – the singers learn not to think. Do you tell your choir that they are singing too loudly when the passage is marked 'soft'? Do you tell them when they aren't blending? Do you tell the tenors that they are singing sharp? Do you tell the altos that they are singing flat? Do you tell the basses that they're singing wrong notes? Do you tell the sopranos, whether they be adults or children, that they breathe in the wrong place? Probably you do, for you think that's what you are there to do.

But then you wonder why they don't remember what you told them by the time Sunday comes. You must find a better way of leading your rehearsal so that they will remember.

Teach them through questions

The great secret, which a few do know but many don't, is to get your singers to tell you what it is that you want to tell them. You do this by asking them the right questions.

If you have to tell your choir that they are singing loudly when the passage is marked 'soft', it's because they know jolly well that you have always taken responsibility for their singing with correct expression – and so they don't bother to think about it for themselves. You have to find a way to give that responsibility to them.

So say to them, 'You may care to look at the expression mark at the top of the page.' You are then encouraging them to look at the music intelligently and to do something about it. But simply because you've drawn their attention to something that they ought to have noticed doesn't mean that they will do it right first time. So then you ask, 'Was that really soft? Sing it again.' And almost certainly it won't be as soft as you want, so you insert a little humour into the situation, after their second attempt, by saying, 'If the composer had wanted it sung with a mushy *mf* he'd have written 'mushy *mf*' in the score, but he didn't. So do what he wrote.'

(Touches of humour are essential during intensive rehearsals, for they are an infallible means of recharging everyone's batteries instantly, including yours.)

And so, by the third attempt they'll sing it well, without you once telling them to sing it softly.

Singers need to correct their own faults

It's the same with every facet of choir training. If the tenors can't hear that they are sharp (and because you had to tell them that they were sharp you implied that they didn't know) they will probably sing sharp on Sunday. They have to correct their own faults right now, so that they will be able to correct themselves on Sunday – because you won't be able to correct them during the service.

And so you ask them, 'Tenors, were you sharp or flat on that note?' Then you play their note on the piano, and they have to think. (Probably they've never had to think about this before – it will be a new experience.) Once you've got the right answer, get them to sing that one note really in tune. Then sing the few notes beforehand which lead up to that note, because they have to know what it feels and sounds like to approach that faulty note.

You can use this method in every situation, instead of merely telling singers their faults. It helps them to discover their faults for themselves, and so remember them.

Here are some more questions:

Basses, are you singing all the Ds in 'God so loved the world'?

Sopranos, were you sharp or flat on that note?

Choir, did we all start that first chord absolutely together?

Did you begin that crescendo too loudly or too softly?

Did you sing that note for its full length?

Where did you breathe in that phrase?

Where shouldn't you breathe? (Same answer)

And so where should you breathe?

Get them to make at least two further attempts to sing it better. Having them do it only once means that your standards aren't high enough, and your choir will not have experienced the thrill of singing that passage better than they thought they could.

Teaching children

This technique of teaching by asking questions is especially appropriate when rehearsing children. Young children need to talk (ask any parent). And so enable them to talk by asking them a question every fifteen seconds. This will stimulate their lively interest in everything you do. Ask simple questions, which everyone can answer, such as:

What's the name of the first note – A or B?

How many beats – one or two? What does the time signature mean?

How many beats' rest are there before you come in?

Choir, what was wrong there?

Did we all start together?

Where shouldn't you breathe in that line?

Where did you breathe? (Same answer!)

Where will you breathe? Let's try it.

Who was right? Sing it for us, Fred . . . well done!

How many beats should there be on that note?

Who can sing it correctly? Mary, you try.

Well done, that was nearly right.

What was the slight problem? Try it once more.

So let your questions be two-pronged: 'Is it A, or is it B?', 'How many beats are there in a minim? Is it one, or is it two?' And if someone gives the wrong answer, always say, 'Nearly – try again.' This will enable the child to give the right answer and to be rewarded with a smiling 'Well done' from you. She will then 'possess' the right answer for herself and sing it right on Sunday. A 'No' in response to a wrong answer tends to be a put down: 'You're wrong – let's find someone better than you to give the right answer.' So always try to help them to get it right.

Teaching adults

With adult choirs the questions should be less frequent, for that would indeed be treating them like children. On the other hand they do need to be encouraged to think. Some of the questions listed above would be appropriate for adults, but not all of them require an answer, for they'll all realise that their first attempt was not good enough; and so you can go ahead with a second attempt, with everyone knowing what they ought to do.

Memorable numbers

There are scientifically proven statistics about people's ability to remember:

If you tell them – only 20 per cent remember.

If they tell you (by answering your questions) – 70 per cent remember.

If they tell you and DO it – 90 per cent remember, and when they do it yet again – even more remember.

Remember, when you get your choir to make a second or third attempt to sing something better, never conduct them more vigorously – for it is they who must make more effort, not you.

And never tell your choir at rehearsal, 'On Sunday, *remember* . . .', because 80 per cent will forget, and now you know why.

CHAPTER 10

An inspiring experience – Miss Marjorie Thomas

Asking the right questions

Before I moved to America it was my privilege occasionally to adjudicate at music festivals throughout Great Britain. I used to enjoy those experiences enormously, for I learned so much from the musicians who performed for me. A fellow adjudicator at one large music festival was a very gracious lady – Marjorie Thomas. She had just retired from being the foremost mezzo-soprano soloist in England and I felt privileged to be on the same adjudicating team with her. She was leading a master class for singers one morning which I wanted to attend; and so when my own class had finished I rushed over to the hall where her class was being held. I arrived just as a singer was returning to his seat, and so I sat at the back of the hall and got out my notebook and pencil to write down everything I could learn from Miss Thomas.

She was sitting on a chair next to the grand piano on a low platform at one end of the hall, and she looked at the audience and said, 'Right, Michael, would you like to come and sing for us?' I wrote in my notebook, 'She knows his name.' That was the first important lesson I learned. She had taken the trouble to find out who her singers were and, by learning their names, she was able to begin communicating with them far more readily than if she just said, 'Next, please.'

Michael walked up to the platform – he was a tall, gangling tenor and obviously very nervous. He looked at the pianist, cleared his throat and began to sing – not very well, I'm afraid. After he'd finished his song there was polite applause from the audience, and I wondered what on earth Miss Thomas could say to him publicly, for he clearly needed a lot of help.

She looked at him very encouragingly and said, 'Well, Michael, what was your song about?' He looked a little puzzled and said, 'It's about a young man and a young woman and they're in love.' 'Yes,' she replied, 'and what happens in the first verse?' He thought for a few seconds and said, 'The young man says so-and-so to the young woman.' 'Quite right, Michael, but what do you think he's really thinking deep down?' This really challenged him, and so he thought for a while and then he said, 'I expect he's thinking such-and-such.'

She then asked him what the second verse was all about (it was the young lady's reply to her young man) and asked Michael what he felt she was really thinking. Michael clearly hadn't thought out the implications of what he was singing, and so Miss Thomas's questions really made him look deeply into the meaning of the song. And so she took him through every verse and encouraged him to recreate in his own mind what was really going on between those two.

She didn't give him any helpful hints as to how he could improve his vocal technique. No! After asking him those basic, searching questions about the meaning of the song, all she said was, 'Right, Michael, sing your song for me again.' And Michael sang his song again; but, my word, what a difference there was! When he sang the young man's verses he bristled with masculinity, and when he sang the young lady's replies he was delicate and sensitive. It was a magnificent performance which brought the whole song to life, and he received a tumultuous ovation from the audience.

But how much had Miss Thomas told him to inspire him to change his interpretation so dramatically? She had told him nothing whatsoever! All she had done was to draw out of him what she knew was already within him, but which he hadn't realised was there. I was lost in amazement at what she had achieved solely by asking the right questions. She could never have achieved such a transformation however much technical information she had given him about vocal production. I've never forgotten that experience, for it changed my whole approach to teaching.

When I work with children, be they young or more experienced, I ask a question every fifteen seconds. When working with adults, I may ask a question every twenty or thirty seconds. I led some choral workshops recently for the Royal College of Organists. Half of the musicians present were school music teachers. One evening I demonstrated how readily children can respond when, through frequent questions, they are invited to participate actively in the learning process. ('Show me how you should hold your music.' 'Did we all really begin together?' 'There was a wrong note there – what was it? Who can sing it correctly for me?' 'Did we start that crescendo too loudly or too softly?') At our next class one teacher told us that she'd tried this technique with her children and that it had worked. 'They'd never sung so well for me!' she enthused.

If you are a really dynamic conductor who can hold the full attention of your choir for ninety minutes non-stop, then perhaps you needn't ask so many questions. Instead you could phrase your remarks by saying, 'Would you agree that you weren't singing together?' That way you are still drawing them into the decision-making process, and thus giving the responsibility for singing to them, rather than taking it upon yourself.

When singers – be they children or adults – have been with me for only a couple of practices, I even begin to ask the question, 'What am I going to ask you now?' or 'You know what you should have done there – so show me'; for I try to run my rehearsals as educational programmes. There's no need to tell your singers all the time what to correct if you've taught them properly, for that's a certain way of ensuring that they don't listen to you.

Asking the right questions is an infallible way of ensuring that your singers remember to do on Sundays what they rehearsed during the week, because they will have learned what to do for themselves. My debt to Miss Thomas for what she taught me that morning is immense, and it will work for you too.

CHAPTER 11

Stop your singers talking

The discipline of concentration

If some of your singers tend to start talking as soon as they've stopped singing, you need to do something about it; because if they're talking, they can't be concentrating on what you want from them, and they can't be listening to the instructions you're giving them.

Talking during rehearsals may be usual in some choirs, but it certainly isn't helpful – to you or to them. A singer who talks is generally a singer who doesn't care, or who hasn't yet experienced the thrill of concentrating for long periods to achieve a really worthwhile musical goal. This applies to all singers – to children, to young people and to adults.

Never think that, because your singers are all volunteers you can't expect a disciplined response from them by stopping them from talking. Would a sports coach allow such inattention? Certainly not. If you want to train your singers to become an integral and important part of a superb choir, you must discover how to stimulate their total attention for long periods. They will thank you for it.

If choir directors, not only of children's choirs but also of adult choirs, think more like sports coaches, albeit less aggressively, they'll find that their singers will respond with increasing eagerness to the challenges that they are given as they find their technique improving week by week.

This involves three things –

1. Give your singers the thrill and satisfaction of achieving high standards by being wholly committed yourself to the music and to the singers. You really have to care deeply that your choristers shall sing this music as well as they possibly can. At every practice, stretch them just a little beyond what they think they're capable of.

2. Present your singers with worthwhile music. A diet of hymns or simple songs will work for a little while, but they will need stronger meat if they are going to turn up for every rehearsal.

3. Be a congenial companion to all your singers, young and old. Exude friendship and conviviality at all times.

When I was in Princeton, I found that two of my teenage singers, both proficient in schoolwork and also in games, actually volunteered to give up tennis and swimming for a season so that they could sing in my choirs. I had become a musical 'sports coach' to them because of my wholehearted commitment to them as people and to the challenging music they sang.

Once you begin to lead your practices in a commanding way – with lots of good humour – and once you speak only when you have something worthwhile to say, ensuring that every instruction you give is immediately followed by an active response from all your singers, you will begin to find that this tendency to chatter will gradually die out. Your singers will respect you more and will want to please you, because you speak with authority.

Chatter-breaks

You may have to mention this tendency to chatter to them if it persists, for they may not be aware that it is getting in the way of your efficiently run rehearsal. Equally, it's important that you do occasionally allow your singers time to relax. It's all a question of balance. Give your energetic adolescents a chatter-break every fifteen minutes. Stand alongside them and join in the conversation, showing that it's OK to relax for a minute or so. Adult singers would welcome a short break every thirty or forty minutes, perhaps, to allow notices to be given out.

A faulty approach

Don't make the mistake of talking over those chattering singers, or trying to talk more loudly than they do. This situation should not be a battle of wills – theirs against yours. There are more of them than there are of you, and so they will always win, and you will always lose. If you allow this situation to go on too long, you are, in effect, giving them permission to go on talking while you are talking – even though you say many times, 'Please don't talk.'

I once saw a conductor lead a practice of a national choral society. Every time she stopped the choir to make a point, several of her singers started to talk. And so every time she stopped the singing she said, 'Shush – don't talk,' but the chatterers took no notice. I couldn't believe what I saw. She said it so automatically that she didn't realise she was doing it – and it had no effect whatsoever. The singers continued to talk, because she didn't wait for them to stop. It was as if she was giving them permission to talk.

An effective approach

This is how you can stop your singers from talking –

1. Be determined

You can begin to do it almost immediately, if you have the determination to see it through.

2. Be strong

Summon up the inner strength which will enable you to face this situation head-on – but do it graciously and with enormous self-control.

3. Be precise

You need to believe that everything you say to your choir is worth their full attention. This is not being big-headed, for if what you say to your singers is not worth their full attention, don't say it. But if you wish to correct a fault – the choir has been singing too loudly, or there are some wrong notes to put right, or the balance is bad, or whatever – then the whole choir needs to pay attention to what you are saying. One reason you may have allowed this situation to go uncorrected is because you didn't really believe in your heart of hearts that what you wanted to say was really worth everyone's total attention.

4. Use the power of silence

Next time chattering breaks out while you're speaking, stop talking yourself and wait patiently until the chatterers have finished – giving them a quietly smiling glance so that the rest of the choir will know what you are doing. After they have stopped, let there be three seconds (that's a long time) of silence. Silence is one of the most powerful tools in the matter of attaining discipline, as every school-teacher knows.

5. Remind them of the importance of worthwhile rehearsals

Say something like this: 'I know that we all want to make this practice worthwhile – for you've all left your comfortable homes to be here tonight, and I appreciate that so much. But to make it really worthwhile you will agree that we need to work as efficiently as possible in rehearsing our music. You'll also agree that, for us all to sing together, we need to work together on correcting details – starting together, singing right notes expressively, and so on. And finally, you'll agree that it makes it difficult for all of us to improve, when not everyone listens to what I say.'

6. Establish a clear goal

Everyone will know what you're getting at by now, and so you take a deep breath and deliver the punchline: 'And so you will agree that it would be helpful if only one person talks at a time when we're rehearsing. Generally that will be me, but if anyone else wants to make a point, I'll be happy to listen – and so will we all.'

7. Maintain goodwill

Smile when you say all this, for your discipline will only work through your singers' goodwill. You cannot repri-mand adults, for that would be demeaning to them and to you. This is true whether you are older or younger than your singers. Courtesy must always rule your approach to your choir when they talk, when they sing flat or are late. Your currency for positive action in your choir is goodwill, and you must promote and foster that at every opportunity. A smile is worth a hundred words of praise. A smile, from the heart, will release a flood of goodwill from the singers to you. A genuine smile will show that you love them – and that's the greatest asset you can have.

8. Use peer pressure

You will have noticed that I suggest that you say, 'You will agree', rather than, 'I think'. In other words, you are not exercising your own authority, which you have only because your adult singers allow you to have it, but you are using peer pressure. It will be the other singers who will put pressure on the chatterers to fall into line, not you.

9. Wait

And so, next time someone talks – and they will, because they've done it for so long – stop talking yourself, and wait until they've finished. Again, with a smile and a raised eyebrow, draw the other adults into the situation by your glance. If you show strong self-control at these moments, and don't show impatience, you will find that some of your other adult singers will begin to 'shush' the talkers, and not you. The other singers will get annoyed at the talkers (if you maintain your courteous, silent approach) and it is they who will supply the necessary pressure to get them to stop, for the talkers will be seen to be wasting everyone's time.

10. Make listening worthwhile

When everyone does eventually give you their full atten-tion, make sure that what you have to say is really worth listening to, otherwise there will be no point in what you have done and ill-feeling will result. In other words, realise that this is a big step, and make sure you're ready to take it.

Talking children

When children talk in your practices you may be more direct in your approach. But if you have gained the confidence and affection of your young singers (and there's no other way to lead a children's choir) still use peer pressure and creative silence to check their talking. You might ask the children to raise their hands when they want to say something. This will help to add more order, and thus more efficiency and more fun, into your children's choir – for children really do prefer order to disorder.

Don't fall into the trap of giving unco-operative children repeated opportunities to amend their behaviour, for this will show that you don't really mean it when you ask them to stop talking. 'William, please stop talking.' 'William, I asked you to stop talking.' 'William, I shan't tell you again to be quiet.' 'William, how many more times must I tell you to behave?' William knows very well that he is in charge of the situation, and not you.

Using peer pressure and the power of silence will go a long way to control this situation. (See Chapter 12 for more on this subject.)

There's a direct correlation between your enthusiasm for the music you are rehearsing, and the enthusiasm shown by your singers – be they adults or children. If you have prepared your music before your rehearsal so that you know, very clearly, what it is that you want to teach, your singers will respond to your leadership with equal commitment. If, on the other hand, you wonder why your singers are unresponsive, it may be because you have little or nothing to teach them.

Of course, the best way to ensure that you always have co-operative singers in your choir is to make your rehearsals challenging and creative experiences, as well as having a friendly attitude to every chorister. This, in a nut-shell, is what this book is all about: *Love the music with all your heart, and love your singers as yourself.*

What this means in practice is that, when you love the music with all your heart, you will automatically have the inner compulsion to enthuse your choir to sing it superbly. And when you love your singers as yourself, you will want each one of them, eventually, to experience the thrill of singing it far better than they could ever imagine.

I heard a story recently of a parent who was asked, at the last minute, to referee his small son's football match because the regular referee would be late. He didn't want to do it, because he had no idea what the rules were. His little son told him what he should do, but he really didn't get a grip on the situation, and so he found himself in the middle of a field with a gang of little boys who quickly took advantage of his indecision, and as a result chaos reigned. But nobody was really enjoying the game.

Fortunately, the regular referee turned up after fifteen minutes and restored order. He told the boys where the boundary was, what the rules were and that everyone should obey him. This meant that the boys were now free to enjoy their game.

Dr Noel Rawsthorne, former director of music of Liverpool Cathedral, has said, 'Discipline can be fun. Singing is fun, playing the organ is fun, conducting can be fun – and they all need discipline.' Tennis attracts enthusiastic players because its boundaries are so clearly defined. The players know that when they play within those simple boundaries they can excel – and the standard they achieve through self-discipline and concentrated effort is thrilling. The same boundaries of self-discipline can apply to one's choir – be they children or adults – and they will enjoy every challenge you give them when your enthusiasm for the music and your helpful, friendly attitude to them, individually and corporately, are always apparent.

The children in all my choirs have been free to enjoy every minute of our rehearsals, because they knew that the rules were there to help them achieve thrillingly high standards. Once they discovered that, they gained a measure of self-discipline which helped them and will continue to help them for the rest of their lives. One of the head boys in my volunteer cathedral choir in England is now a Lieutenant-Commander in the Royal Navy. He learned about self-discipline when he was in my choir, and he looks back on those formative years with gratitude and pride. I am enormously proud of him too.

CHAPTER 12

Keep your
singers in order

The problem of disobedient singers

Some choir directors find it difficult to keep good order in their choirs, especially in children's and young people's choirs. Their singers won't do as they're told. They won't sing a phrase in one breath, they won't stand up straight, they won't take trouble with clarity of diction, and they talk incessantly. 'Keeping order' is a skill which many of us have had to learn through painful experience.

Give choirs responsibility for their own singing

Some conductors seem to take full responsibility for the singing of their choirs, and yet the singers still don't follow their instructions. I heard a small choir recently, made up of very well-trained young ladies. Their conductor was their singing teacher, who had a strong personality. But when they sang their songs, even though the tone was beautiful, they kept on taking breaths in the middle of phrases. I was surprised. When I met their conductor after their performance I mentioned this, and she said, with gracious forcefulness, 'I keep on telling them not to breathe in the middle of phrases, but they don't take any notice.'

The problem was that, as she had such a strong personality, her singers felt no sense of personal responsibility for their own singing. Instead of trying to impose her own personality on the choir, she should have recognised that it wasn't she who was going to sing those songs, but the members of her choir; and so she should have given the responsibility for the singing to her singers.

She could have done that, as we saw in Chapter 9, by asking the singers to tell her what they did incorrectly, and saying, 'Well, do something about it! Let's try it again.'

The same applies to conductors who *don't* have forceful personalities, or who may find it especially difficult to 'keep order' with children and young people. Once the singers realise that the responsibility is theirs, then, more often than not, they will accept that responsibility if they are challenged to do so. Many of us respond to a challenge. So the conductor could say, 'Did we all start together?', 'Did everyone sing that final note for four beats, or only some singers?'

'Keeping order'

Try this method when you want your singers to stand up straight: don't say, 'Stand up straight,' but give the responsibility to them by saying, 'Show me how you should stand when you're singing'. Some of the singers will stand up straight, but not the others. What should you do then?

Ah, now that's where you need to exercise a bit of 'keeping order' technique! What you should *not* do is take any notice *whatsoever* of the children who are not standing up straight – not even throwing them a glance.

Instead, you should look at the singers who *are* standing well and praise them, with genuine appreciation: 'That's great, you are standing well. Thank you.'

As for the children who are *not* standing up straight, the main reason why they are being so difficult is to get your attention. So-called naughty children are a pain because they want the teacher's attention, and the surest way to get it is to be a bit of a pain. So don't play their game. If you give your total attention to the children who are doing what you want, the other children will gradually get the message. And when the unhelpful child finally decides to stand up straight, don't forget to give him or her an encouraging smile and say, 'Well done!' – but not, 'Well done, and about time too!'

It will take a lot of self-control on your part to ignore the uncooperative singers – all they want from you is a quick glance of disapproval to show that you've noticed them, so don't even give them that satisfaction.

If you persevere with this technique, you'll find that it will work. But if you expect a child to be unco-operative, that child will know, and your expectation will be fulfilled.

A positive attitude

The great secret for creating good order in your children's choir is actively to cultivate a positive liking for each and every one of the children – even the so-called naughty ones. Work at becoming their friend and taking an active interest in their interests – their sporting activities, their hobbies and their families. Once a child feels that you don't like him (which means, in effect, that you are afraid of him) you won't be able to do anything with him.

But you are an adult, therefore you have a stronger personality than a child. Use your stronger personality to radiate love – or respect and goodwill – to every child, before, during and after your rehearsal.

Disruptive children

Occasionally a child's inattention may lead to inappropriate behaviour. When this happens it's important to deal with it both firmly and positively.

And so when a child's behaviour begins to get in the way of the other children, give that child one clear warning: 'William, you are annoying the other children. If you do that again, you must leave the room.'

Note that (a) William's behaviour is annoying his peers, not you; he doesn't mind annoying you, but he does mind annoying his peers. And (b) exclusion from the group is one of the most effective punishments.

When he misbehaves again, as he surely will, do not move the goal posts, i.e. do not give him another chance, because that will enable him to think, 'I wonder how many times I can get away with it before she sends me out.' It will have become a game between you, and he holds the aces.

Instead, deal with this situation positively by showing him that he has to control his own behaviour. 'William, you're still annoying the other children, and so you must leave the room. When you decide that you want to join in with the rest of us, you may come back again. It's your decision.'

And so, when he does return it must be on terms of total forgiveness and welcome on your part – like the welcome given to the Prodigal Son. There must be no trace of: 'I shall be watching you to see if you misbehave again.' He must be accepted back within the full fellowship of the group as though he had never misbehaved.

On the other hand, if his behaviour continues to be a problem to you, to the choir and to himself, you need to exercise the ultimate sanction: 'Tell your parents I shall be coming to see them.' (See Chapter 26)

Homework

Leading a well-organised practice means homework. Before you go to your rehearsal, actively gear up your mind to think, 'I really love all those children – and I'll show it by my friendly attitude to them all at tonight's rehearsal.' If you persist in this attitude, you'll be happily surprised at the results you reap.

I find that carefully prepared warm-ups, which involve deep breathing, can transform unruly attitudes in children, and quickly make them ruly! They're a most effective way to instil order amongst adults too.

CHAPTER 13

Watch out for the second law of thermodynamics

If left to themselves, choirs always forget much of what you've told them, and slip back into bad habits – they don't stand up straight, they don't watch their conductor, they talk instead of listening to instructions. This comes under the second law of thermodynamics – which Dr Freeman Dyson, one of my choir parents in the USA, defined as 'entropy increases'.

This means that it takes more energy to put something right than it did for it to go wrong. It takes more energy to tidy a room than it did to make it untidy. And so choir practices often involve putting right this week something that you already put right last week.

The leading of practices is like pushing a man up a greasy pole. He goes up with a bit of effort, but slides down naturally when you leave him alone. And so this means that, unless you continually push your choir, challenging them to sing better every week, their standards will inevitably fall. The greasy pole doesn't only apply to choirs, but also to us choral directors. If I'm not leading my choir better this week than I did last week, I need to do something about it. Things left to their own devices deteriorate – it's the second law of thermodynamics.

Or, putting it another way, your choir will get away with whatever you let them get away with. It's human nature; it's a manifestation of original sin to get away with whatever we can. When you're driving your car and see a police car in your rear-view mirror you slow down, but when the police car has gone you speed up again, and maybe break the speed limit. It's the authority figure that stops you.

It's the same with your choir. They will sit or stand in a slovenly manner, unless they see that good stance is really important to you. And you'll have to remind them of this at least three times during every practice. If you mention it only once at the beginning of your rehearsal – 'Show me how well you can stand when singing' – they will do it; but after a few minutes, some will have relapsed to a lazy stance. And if you don't push them up that greasy pole immediately, they will continue to slide down.

The second law of thermodynamics is alive and very well in every detail of every rehearsal you lead: right notes, correct breathing, intonation, blend and balance, diction, watching the conductor . . . and on and on.

CHAPTER 14

Ten basic musical points for every rehearsal

1. Singing the right notes

This is what every choir director wants, and what every singer wants – so here's how you can achieve it.

(a) Define the fault exactly

Stop the choir when you hear a wrong note, and define exactly what the fault is: 'Tenors, you sang an F there instead of an E,' It's no good saying, 'Tenors, you made a mistake there. Do it again.' For they will do it again, and it'll still be wrong, because they don't know what the fault is – you haven't told them.

Similarly, it's no good telling a choir that they're singing out of tune; they don't know if they're sharp or flat, and they don't know if it's the basses or the sopranos who are out of tune, and they don't know which note is out of tune. Choir directors must define, very precisely, what the fault is, and then your singers, with your help, can begin to do something about correcting it.

(This doesn't contradict what I said in Chapter 9 about the importance of singers correcting their own faults. When you have trained them in all the skills I shall deal with in this chapter, that's exactly what they will be able to begin to do.)

(b) Put that one fault right

Take that one note and get the tenors to sing it – just that one E to that one word. Your singers need to know what the note should sound like if they're trying to sing correctly, so make it easy for them – play the note for them. It's essential in a rehearsal to make the music easy for your singers to sing well.

(c) Sing it in context

Then get them to sing a couple of bars, on their own, before that E. There's no such thing as a difficult note – it's the getting to that note which may be difficult. It's the same with playing the piano – all notes, by themselves, are easy. The difficulty lies in being able to get to that note in time and safely. So rehearse the 'getting to' with your singers.

(d) Do it again

If they get it right, say, 'Good – do it again.' When singers have sung a passage correctly once, which they had formerly sung incorrectly, always get them to sing it again. They need to sing it right at least twice, to ensure that it will stay right.

(e) Get the whole choir to join in

Ask the full choir to sing that short passage together, so that the tenors can hear how the right note sounds in context. Thus you will help them to relate what they are singing to what everybody else is singing.

The key to correcting wrong notes is to focus on detail. When you spot a fault and tell the singers what was wrong, don't go back half a page, as some choir directors do. No. First correct the fault precisely where it is, and only then can you begin to go back a short way. It's like mending a puncture in a tyre. Find out where the hole is, and then you can fix the patch exactly over that hole, so that the whole tyre will be mended. You have to be precise when correcting errors.

Explain why the error occurred. Doing your homework will enable you to spot why the tenors sang an F instead of an E. Perhaps the altos had sung an F in the previous bar. Point this out to your tenors, and get the altos to sing their F, followed by the tenors singing their E. Singing correct notes is all about relationships – the relationship of this note to the next one and how we reached it from the one before.

Use time efficiently. The correcting of a wrong note should not take more than, say, thirty seconds, when you concentrate on a tiny detail – i.e. correcting this one note and then singing the notes on either side of it – instead of doing the whole page again. But don't rehearse one voice part on its own for more than a minute, for you'll be wasting the time of the other singers.

Involve most of your singers most of the time. If you have to spend more than a minute in correcting a passage, get the other singers to sing along with your tenors, i.e. employ them, rather than have them 'switch off'. If the passage is too high for the basses to join in, then ask the sopranos only to sing an octave higher with the tenors. Similarly, ask the altos to sing along with the basses when they have an error.

Remember! The longer a wrong note stays uncorrected, the more difficult it is to get it right. Instrumentalists know the truth of this. And so, when your choir is learning a new anthem, getting the notes right in pitch and in rhythm must be your first priority.

2. Correct breathing

Start right

As I've already said in Chapter 8 – when choirs are left to themselves they breathe twice too often. That's why it's so important, when your choir is learning a new anthem, that they should mark where breaths should and should not be taken. If this is not done and is not followed through – by the choir director insisting that everyone breathes where they ought to – it will be almost as difficult to correct as correcting a long-term wrong note.

Much of singing in a choir is to do with automatic reflexes, i.e. singers performing as they have been trained to perform. So the matter of getting things right at the very beginning of the process is vital.

Every adult singer should have a pencil and an eraser to mark their own copies, sparingly, at the conductor's direction. This will, in the long run, save a lot of rehearsal time. Children should not mark copies – they tend to deface their music through over enthusiasm, or misplaced creativity. Mark their copies for them.

Do your homework. The choir will only know where they should breathe if you have done your homework by marking your own copy first.

3. Expressive phrasing

There's a simple way to enable your choir to sing in phrases – to sing with subtle expression so as to bring out the meaning of the words and to make the music sound alive and beautiful. And this is it:

(a) Find the important syllable

In any phrase of words there is one syllable which is more important than any other. Ask your singers what they think is the important syllable in a phrase. When you do, you'll find that they will suddenly take much more interest in the meaning of the words, and thus sing the music so much more beautifully. Look at these examples :

> There is a green hill *far* away.
> My soul doth *mag*nify the Lord.
> Praise, my soul, the *King* of heaven.
> Ave Verum *Cor*pus.
> Since by man came *death*.

(b) *Crescendo* and *diminuendo*

Encourage your choir to *crescendo* gently towards that important syllable and to *diminuendo* away afterwards. You'll find that, at first, they will over stress the important syllable. Encourage them to make their *crescendos* and *diminuendos* really smooth and even.

A choir is essentially an expressive instrument – or it should be. Many choir directors are also organists or pianists. The organ and piano are essentially inexpressive instruments; they cannot really *crescendo* through a note (except somewhat ineffectively on an organ through opening the swell-box or adding stops). Therefore some choir directors may not think in terms of natural phrasing – as a violinist or clarinettist would do. They think of loud or soft, rather than feeling the forward movement *through* a note, or *through* a phrase, so that it becomes a living, breathing, onwards flowing musical experience.

A choir should always *crescendo* or *diminuendo* even when the composer hasn't written in those expression marks – as long as it's subtle. Once expression draws attention to itself rather than to the music, it is overdone.

Look at this example from the beginning of Fauré's *Requiem*. This is written to be sung very softly – and that's all the composer wrote. Many choirs sing it with just a 'straight' *pianissimo*. But look at the words: 'Requiem aeternam'. If you were to speak those words you would naturally stress the second syllable of 'aet-*er*-nam'. And if you say the words with a sense of forward movement towards that syllable – a very subtle *crescendo* towards it and a hardly noticeable *diminuendo* after it – the words immediately become much more alive.

Once a choir has caught the thrill of singing with subtle expression (I used to ask my Princeton choirs to sing in 'curves') they'll find that their performance takes on a whole new way of life.

Of course, there are times when a choir should not make *crescendos* and *diminuendos*. For example, there's a special moment in Fauré's *Requiem* – the *Agnus Dei* – where the sopranos sing a long upper C on the word 'Lux' and the harmonies change from C major to A flat major. It's a magical moment. That long C should be sung 'straight', with no extra expression. And it's so much more effective, sung 'straight', if the other music has been sung with 'curves'.

Though there isn't time for you to tell your choir to put *crescendos* and *diminuendos* in every other bar, once you've asked them to find for themselves where the important syllables are, and once you've rehearsed them in responding to the expressive gestures of your left hand and arm, they will quickly feel the music as deeply as you do, and they'll be able to make subtle changes in the expression as you conduct them creatively – by looking at them and not at your music.

If there's one technique above all others which will transform the singing of your choir, this is it; because it will ensure that –

> your singers are thinking;
> your singers are breathing in the right places;
> your singers are creating music rather than just singing notes;
> your singers understand the meaning of the words and therefore are communicating this meaning to the congregation;
> your singers are more aware of the other singers in your choir, for they will be listening more creatively, and therefore they will tend to blend better and to sing together more readily.

(c) Rehearsing expression

Your singing of a simple hymn could be transformed, by easy stages during your rehearsal, to something like this –

leave   the   gloom - y___ haunts   of   sad - ness.

You might think that is far too complicated, and that your choir would get very confused if you had to rehearse every bar to get the expression and breathing as right as that. But it depends how you do it. Instead of telling them what to do, **ask** them –

First – 'Where will you not breathe?' (Then ask them to sing a few bars.)

Second – 'Where will you breathe?' (Then sing those bars again – perhaps two or three times.)

Third – 'Which is the most important syllable in that phrase? – What should you do, therefore, to bring out its meaning?' Answer: *Crescendo* towards it, and *diminuendo* away from it. 'Right. Let's do it.'(Again, they will have to do it two or three times before everyone feels that they really have achieved what *they* set out to do.)

In this way, *they* will 'own' the interpretation, and they won't be burdened with having to remember the hundred and one things you would have 'told them' to do.

All this applies to most choral music. In romantic music the *crescendos* and *diminuendos* can be a little larger than they would be in, say, the music of Byrd. Let your expression be subtle so that, instead of drawing attention to itself, enhances the meaning of the words and enables the music to live.

Your singing of *Jesu, joy of man's desiring* could be transformed, using this method of 'introducing one challenge at a time':

Je - su, joy____ of man's___ de - sir - ing.

Sing four bars in one breath: make the tiniest break after 'Jesu'.

Most composers don't write all those expression marks into their music; Bach and Byrd certainly didn't; Elgar was one composer who did. I call it, 'discovering hidden expression marks'. You only have to compare it with how an actor will read a passage of prose – he puts in subtle inflexions to bring alive the message of the words. The author expected his words to be brought to life. If words were read as 'flatly' as they are written on the page, they would sound incredibly dull. In the same way, it's up to a choir to bring the music to life with the use of subtle expression which may not be written on the page.

Two examples spring to mind in John Rutter's 'For the beauty of the earth'. The word 'earth' is the most important word in that phrase, therefore crescendo gently towards it. And, as it lasts for two whole bars, once you have reached it, make a one-bar *crescendo,* and then a one-bar *diminuendo.* It will give that word a most musical 'curved' shape. Similarly, in the phrase, 'Lord of all, to thee we raise', *crescendo* from the word 'all' right through to the middle of 'raise'. This will make this lovely music sound even more beautiful.

4. Improving intonation

The sin against the Holy Ghost, musically speaking, is, for me, singing out of tune. A choir can sing all the right notes, with expression and excellent rhythm, but if it is not in tune, it sounds like sour milk! So, in order to deal with this, you must show your choir that singing in tune is important to you.

(a) Get your choir to practise singing in tune

Rehearse them two or three times during your practice, singing one chord, or one note, really well in tune. Thus they'll know that this is something they have to pay attention to. It's all to do with good vocal production, listening creatively to each other and listening to the piano or organ.

One helpful exercise you might like to try is to get your choir to sustain a chord, one note at a time, and tell you if it's really in tune. For example, sing the final chord in the short chorus, 'Since by man came death' (*Messiah*) to the vowel 'Aw' in the following way. (It is so often sung flat. Once the choir knows and experiences how that chord should sound, they will the more easily be able to sing it in tune in context.) The singers may breathe as often as they like to keep that chord going for up to a minute while they listen to each other.

Could be sung down a 3rd in C major

Sung to a continuous 'Aw'

Start with the root – sung by a higher voice, rather than a lower voice, for it's easier to hear at the higher pitch. That note is the foundation of the chord. Once that is being sung absolutely in pitch by all the singers in that particular voice part (and it may not be, to begin with) then you can get the voice which sings the same note at a lower octave to join in. Make sure that everyone is listening really intently to what the other voices are doing, so that they may the more accurately sing their own part in tune. An octave is the easiest interval to pitch.

Then bring in the voice which sings the fifth. This should be sung very slightly sharp.

When the first three notes are being sung in tune, to the satisfaction of you and your choir, bring in the voice which is singing the major third. This is the most difficult note to sing in tune. It, too, should be sung slightly sharp. (Minor thirds should be tuned slightly flat.) I find that the phrase 'window of opportunity' is helpful here. There's only one very narrow place where that one note can fit, and so the singers have to focus very intently to get it right.

Here's another example to encourage your singers to sing really in tune:

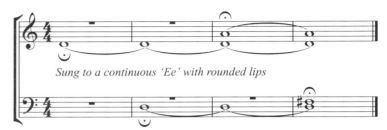

Sung to a continuous 'Ee' with rounded lips

Your singers won't get it right the first time, but you will have begun the process whereby they will get increasingly better at it, week by week, if you persevere. There is a 'rightness' which everyone will appreciate when a chord is sung really well in tune. It's worth striving for – and worth maintaining. Remember the second law of thermo-dynamics: you have to keep pushing the man up that greasy pole.

By the way, you may sometimes have to sing music with an English cadence, or a false relation. They occur fairly frequently in the music of the Byrd period, when you have, for example, a B flat sung in one voice, followed a few notes later (or even simultaneously) by another voice singing a B natural; or an F sharp followed by an F natural. When those moments occur, ask your singers to sing the flat note slightly flatter, and the sharp, or natural note, a fraction sharper. This will make those exquisitely pointed harmonies sound even more delightful.

(b) Advanced intonation

Once your choir really has got the idea of singing chords well in tune, try, during your warm-ups, to get them to sing one fairly low-pitched chord, and then to go up a semitone without a break – breathing as often as they like, except when they change their note. (Play this succession of chords on the piano so that your singers will know what to aim for. But let them sing unaccompanied.)

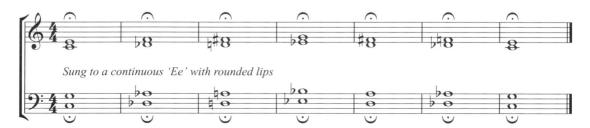

Sung to a continuous 'Ee' with rounded lips

When they have moved from the first chord to the second, they should listen to that new chord, and put up their hands when they think that it's in tune. Then, at your direction, they can go up another semitone, and so on, for three or four chords. Then, still without a break in the sound, they should come down again, one semitone at a time, listening to each chord and staying with it until it's really in tune. And once they've reached their 'home' chord again, check it with the piano. If they're in pitch with the piano, great will be their joy.

If it's *not* in pitch, it will be up to you whether or not to do it all again, or part of it, or to say, 'That was a good try. It'll be even better next week.'

When I made CDs with my Princeton Singers in the USA, I always had them sing this exercise before we started recording to ensure they sang absolutely in pitch for the next two hours. And it always worked, for a choir cannot sing this exercise unless all the singers are listening intently to each other, which is the secret, not only for getting intonation right, but also blend, balance, tone and, to a large extent, breathing.*

5. Improving tone

This is how to train your choir to make an agreeable sound.

(a) Children's choirs

With children, make sure that they sing, generally, with head voice rather than chest voice. If they sing music which is based around middle C and find it difficult to sing more than an octave above that note, they are using their chest voices. When children sing 'pop' songs on their own, they always use their chest voices.

If, on the other hand, you give them warm-ups which start around G above middle C, and go gradually up from there – so that they begin singing downward scales from D and above, gently and easily – you will find that they will eventually be able to sing high notes up to G or A or even higher with their head voices. As with adults, listening to each other is the secret of acquiring blending tone, as well as being taught vocal techniques at every rehearsal.

Young children should not be given music to sing which goes below middle C, because physically they are not equipped to sing those notes. Alas, some music is written for children these days which is far too low – going down to A, or even G, below middle C. In which case, either find more suitable music, or transpose the music up two or three steps.

* See Chapter 17 for some more ideas on how to cure faulty intonation.

Older children of around 11 or 12 years of age can sing lower notes, and if they are well trained they can sing with both their head and their chest voices. However, children who sing with their head voices generally make a pleasanter, more blending sound than children who sing with their chest voices all the time. And they can sing a far greater range of notes if they can use their head voices for higher notes, and their chest voices for the lower ones. Being a child singer is all about singing high notes very easily. Babies can pitch very high notes – they do it naturally. It's only when children are a little older that they seem to be encouraged by some choir directors to sing 'unnaturally'.

(b) Adult choirs

It is more difficult to correct adult singers who don't make a pleasant sound because they have sung that way for so long. Basically you need to get them to sing a little more softly. A helpful technique to remember is that soft singing cures a host of faults. Once your singers sing a little more softly and actively listen to the sound that they and the rest of the choir are making, it's amazing how quickly you can get a beautiful sound from them.

Another problem that some adults have is singing with a too wide *vibrato*. This can ruin the blend and balance of a choir. You can deal with this, again, by asking them to sing a little more softly, so that they blend with the other singers. If you have a soprano with a wide 'wobble' try asking her to sing alto, where her *vibrato* will not be so noticeable. You'll have to be very tactful when suggesting this, for, almost certainly, she'll regard herself as a leading soprano in your choir.

But, basically, it all comes down to vocal production. If you are a trained singer, you will enable your choristers to become trained singers also. I had a marvellous assistant in Princeton who was a trained singer, and he led our adult choir, little by little, week by week, to produce their voices well, and so the sound of the choir became really splendid.

The main points to enable singers of all ages to produce their voices well are:

(i) Stance. The body is the instrument. So when choristers stand or sit well, they have taken a giant leap in the matter of achieving good vocal production.

(ii) Breathing. Breathe deeply, breathe low, keeping your shoulders down. Always have more than enough breath to finish singing a phrase. We've mentioned this already,

but its importance cannot be overstressed. Bring it to the attention of your singers not only when they are singing their warm-ups, but also every five minutes when rehearsing music.

(iii) Relaxation. The body, and especially the head, should be wholly relaxed. A tense throat, for example, immediately produces tight tone. So practise relaxing when doing warm-ups. A deep sigh, breathing out, is a good way to begin. (Deep breathing also lowers one's blood pressure, so I'm reliably informed by a medical friend of mine.)

The jaw should be loose and be able to fall open naturally to provide a mobile mouth, and the lips should be pushed slightly forward too. Look at professional singers on TV – you'll find that their mouths are wonderfully expressive – this helps them to produce a lovely sound.

The back of the throat should also be open. Try yawning, and you'll find that the back of your throat opens up – your uvula is raised and so the sound can come through unhindered. Many choir directors rightly encourage their singers to open their mouths – but don't necessarily realise that the back of their throats should also be opened up. A sure test to see if it is open or shut is to get your singers to sing 'Ah' and then pinch their noses while they are still singing. If the back of their throat is closed, their ears will blow off.

But there's no substitute for choir directors having singing lessons themselves. Even a short course of lessons would be a tremendous help.

6. Singing together

'A choir is a disciplined body of singers.' Choirs can find it the greatest fun to try to sing together if they are challenged in an encouraging way, with a smile. But very few achieve real unanimity. I found, and continue to find with all my choirs that, at the beginning of a practice, they don't come in together – be it with warm-ups or singing a simple hymn. I therefore point this out to them ('Did you *all* start together?') and we try again.

If there is one fault above all others which is shared by most choirs, whether they be large or small, it is that the singers do not all begin the first note together. But if they do it's rarely with any feeling of musical movement.

It will help to correct this fault if you enable your choir to feel the rhythm and the mood of the music they are about to sing by saying, 'One, two, ready, *breathe*!'

There's a special sense of unanimity when all the singers are 'marching in step'. But you'll have to rehearse them in this skill at the beginning of every rehearsal, and many times during your practice, for the greasy pole will have blunted their attack since last week.

The secret is that *all* singers should breathe exactly one beat before they start. And even when this is pointed out to them, some of them still breathe roughly half a beat before they should come in – which is too late. You can liken this to the beginning of a race. It's vitally important that all the runners start exactly together, otherwise it's a false start. It's the same with singers. How can they sing a hymn tune or an anthem together if they can't sing their first chord together? So if you take pains to get the first chord sung unanimously, you will find that your choir will be more conscious of singing the rest of the music together. It has a 'knock-on' effect.

And it has a 'knock-on' effect in another sense too; because if you take trouble with one aspect of choir training when rehearsing this anthem, it will tend to be more accurate in the next anthem. That's what practising in detail is all about: one detail here, another detail there – a different one every thirty seconds or so. And gradually their singing will improve and they'll be excited by what they are achieving with you.

All this applies to the exact length of final notes of phrases as well. Very many singers, including some who may have had professional training, tend to hang on to final notes of phrases, even though they know what their exact lengths should be, and also to sing them too loudly. This is especially true when the last note of a phrase is a short one. You'll have to point this out to your choristers time and time again (or, better still, ask them, 'Was that last note too long or too short; too loud or too soft?') Get them, consciously, to sing that final note even shorter than its written length, especially when it is set to a word which has a weak final syllable, such as '*Sav*-iour', 're-*gard*-ed', 'sal-*va*-tion'.

So the achieving of unanimity applies to every facet of choral training.

7. A sense of rhythm

If there's one thing that separates good choirs from inadequate choirs it is the matter of rhythm. If you listen really carefully to a choir singing an anthem in church you will almost certainly notice that they nearly always come in late, especially if the anthem is accompanied. It's generally only a matter of being half a beat late, but it does show that the singers are not feeling the music rhythmically, but only as a succession of notes.

(a) Make a rhythmic start

We have already seen in the previous section of this chapter ('Singing Together') the importance of starting together where I outlined the technique of taking a breath exactly one beat before the start. You can reinforce this with the following exercise, using *Jesu, joy of man's desiring*:

For the second time, don't play these two bars before the choir comes in, but have them count out loud rhythmically, and breathe exactly one beat before they sing.

Get your singers to count two empty bars of rests immediately before they are due to sing, and have them breathe exactly one beat before they start singing: 'One, two, three; two, two, (breathe), *Jesu, joy* . . .'. Almost certainly they still won't all be right, so play four bars before they are due to sing, and have them count the last two bars again, without you playing them. That way they really will feel a sense of corporate rhythm.

One most practical tip to get your choir to start phrases rhythmically and punctually is to put the consonant *before* the beat, so that the vowel comes *on* the beat. This is particularly true of words which begin with 'f', 'h', 'l', 'm', 'n', 'r', 's' and 'th' – such as '*Fff*or the beauty of the earth', '*H*oly, holy, holy . . .', '*Lll*ord, now lettest thou . . .', '*Mmm*y soul doth magnify the Lord', '*Rrr*ejoice, the Lord is king' (get your singers to roll or 'trill' their Rs here), '*Nnn*ow the green blade rises', '*Sss*ince by man came death', '*Ss*steal away to Jesus', *Th*is is the day . . .'. When choirs are encouraged to sing like that, their unanimity and attacks improve beyond belief.

(b) Get them to feel the rhythmic pulse

Choir directors who have a very strong sense of rhythm are able to convey this to their singers. It's not something that can be explained very easily in words – it has to be experienced.

Let me give you an example. Some choirs sing Stainer's *God so loved the world* as though it were just a succession of chords, rather like this:

To get your choir to feel the rhythmic pulse, have them sing a few bars like this, counting the beats to 'one, two, three':

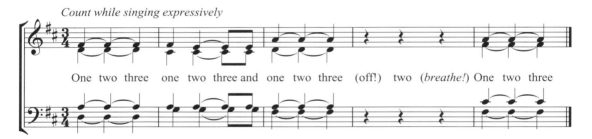

You might even get them to sing those numbers with a sense of religious fervour, i.e. singing them as though they were the words that Stainer set. You may be surprised at how beautiful they can sound. Then, when they return to singing the original words they will find that they have so much more meaning – and that in itself makes the exercise worth doing.

But then, try singing the notes very staccato. This will really sharpen their sense of forward rhythmic flow – and you will find that it's a good exercise to enable the singers to sing really well together. You and they will notice that their concentration increases by leaps and bounds, which again, is a very good thing for them to experience.

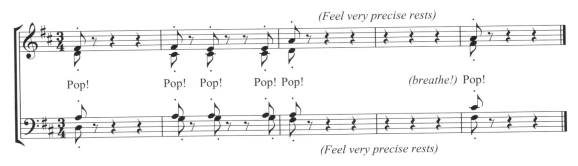

If your choir can sing polyphonic motets, I know of no method which will more surely boost their concentration than singing the notes, very staccato, to 'pop'. You'll find that they'll break down in helpless laughter after they've sung a few bars, so let them laugh, and then try it again for a page. This way they will really feel that the notes have an exact (not an approximate) rhythmic place, so that the next plucked note will start really together.

After this, let them sing the words as smoothly and as clearly as they can, and you'll find that their concentration and focus will, once again, have improved by leaps and bounds.

Another helpful exercise is to sing the notes in repeated quavers to 'Lah' – for instance, the first note in *Jesu, joy . . .*, which is a minim, could be turned into four staccato quavers, and so on. This will again give them a sense of ongoing rhythm which moves through the music, instead of just singing one note after another.

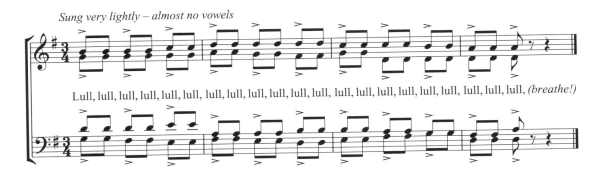

(c) Other rhythmic points

Dotted quaver-semiquaver rhythms also need special care. They can so easily turn themselves into lazy triplets. It's sometimes helpful to sing the dotted quaver slightly *staccato*, in other words, turning those two notes into 'quaver, semiquaver rest, semiquaver'. Make the final semiquaver light – some singers tend to stress it, which makes it too long.

Triplets are sometimes sung too quickly. Stress the first note of a triplet and the others will tend to fall into place.

8. Clear diction

Clarity of diction is something else that can't be mentioned too often. If you, as a choral director, don't make a point of it at least once in every piece you rehearse – 'I can't understand the words you're singing', or 'What letter did you miss out of that word?' – then your choir's diction will quickly deteriorate. The spoken word does, in any case, deteriorate over time. My grandmother, for example, spoke more clearly than I do and, going further back in history, words such as 'salvation' used to be pronounced 'sal-vay-see-on'. That's deteriorated now to an acceptable 'sal-vay-shn'.

Once you've decided that you want your choir to sing words precisely, you will notice obvious faults you have to correct.

(a) Consonants

Last week my village church choir should have sung 'God is kind', but what they actually sang was, 'God is kine'. I asked them to listen very carefully to what they were singing and to tell me what they heard. One bass did spot it, and so they were able to correct the fault for themselves. That, as you know, is the best way to encourage your choir to remember on Sunday what they rehearsed on Friday.

If you have trained your choir to concentrate on very fine detail, there is no limit to the clarity of diction which you can inspire them to achieve. For example, consonants at the ends of words can become so beautiful. Instead of singing, 'Lornow lettucethouthy servandepar tinpeace' (running the words together), you could, with patience, eventually get them to sing, 'Lllord(uh) nnnow lllettest(uh) thou thy servant(uh) depart in peace', making sure that the 'uh' is as small as possible, i.e. not 'Lorder, now lettester . . .'. It mustn't become mannered.

I tried this recently when I guest-conducted a school choir, and they quickly saw what was needed. They enjoyed the challenge by pointing out to me when other words could be treated in a similar way, such as, 'In(uh) the hour of my distress . . .', '. . . and(uh) my spirit . . .' and 'Grrreater lllove hath nnno mman(uh) than(uh) this.'

That's another example of the 'knock-on' effect. They applied, on their own initiative, what they had just learned in one anthem to the next. When that happens to a choir (and it can happen to the most amateur as well as to the most highly trained choirs) one's rehearsals become an exciting time of shared exploration.

The danger of singing consonants clearly is a tendency to transfer the final consonant from the end of one word to the beginning of the next:

> 'We three kings of Orien Tar'
> 'Was to certain poor shepher Dzin fields . . .'
> 'World with ow Ten. Darmen.'

Beware also of the intrusive 'R':

> 'Here Rizza little door'
> 'O Saviour Rov the world'

These faults will need correcting delicately, for they must never be sung pedantically.

Singing consonants clearly takes energy. You'll find that you continually have to galvanise your choir into putting more effort into singing consonants. You ask them, 'What letter did you miss out in the word "anD"'? (for instance) and get them to do it more than once before you are satisfied, for the letter 'd' can so often be replaced by the letter 't'. ('Worlt without ent'). The way to overcome this is to get your singers to experience that a note may be sung on a 'd' but not on a 't'. ('Sing a *staccato* downwards scale to the letter "d": d(uh), d(uh), d(uh) . . .' They'll find that they can't sing a similar scale on a 't'. But make sure that when they do sing the final 'd' of a word ('LorD', 'GoD'), the pitch of that 'd' is the same note as on the word itself. Some singers unconsciously tend to change the pitch on final 'd's. Therefore ask them to sing the word once with an overstressed 'd' ('LorDER', 'GoDER'), so that they can hear the final note more clearly. After that, ask them to lighten it ('LorDuh', 'GoDuh').

(b) Vowels

If your choristers sing with different regional accents, their singing will tend to sound out of tune. It's so important that all their vowels agree. This, again, comes back to you to show them exactly how this or that word should be pronounced, and what they should do with their lips to ensure that it happens.

When my Princeton Singers were singing Choral Evensong in London's St Paul's Cathedral, one member of the congregation told me afterwards that it was not until they began to say the creed that he realised they were an American choir. I'd taught them to sing English music with an English accent!

The main object of singing with clear diction is to bring the words alive, not only to the singers but also to the congregation. The composer wrote the music, having been inspired by the words – so make not only the music, but also the words, inspiring, and very clear.

9. Word stress

Words should be sung with the same stress that they are given when being spoken. But they are not always sung like that, especially by church choirs which tend to linger on final syllables, such as 'Sav-IOUR', 'regar-DED' and 'handmai-DEN.' Think, for example, how some choirs sing responses and hymns: 'And with thy spi-RIT', 'And grant us thy salva-SHUN', 'Great is thy faithful-NESS', 'Dear Lord and Father OF mankind'. All this does violence to the beauty of the English language.

You can teach your choir to sing these syllables properly. Ask them to read the words with natural stress, e.g. 'SAV-iour', 're-GARD-ed', 'HAND-maid'n', etc., and so work out for themselves how they should be sung. Then ask them to monotone them, and then to sing them in context. They'll almost certainly need the statutory three attempts to get them right before you and they are satisfied. And you may also need to give them a little extra help by suggesting that they may want to make final, weak syllables not only softer but shorter.

By the way, the most common vowel in the English language is not an 'e' but the 'schwa'. This is an indeterminate vowel which is pronounced rather like 'uh'. You can find examples everywhere, especially in the word 'the' ('by the way'), as well as many other words: 'handmaiden' ('handmaid'n'), 'servant' ('ser-vuhnt'), 'saviour' ('save-iuh'). Occasionally, when singers are trying very hard to enunciate clearly, they might pronounce 'saviour' as 'save-your'. This is an example of misdirected enthusiasm.

Here is a less obvious example of how words should not be stressed. Think of Stainer's setting of *God so loved the world*. Choirs tend to stress the word 'so' here. But if you try *saying* the words, the stress falls on the word 'loved' – 'God so LOVED the world.'

Once your choir has discovered this for themselves, get them to sing it like that, and they'll find that the music, and the words, come alive as never before. The choir should make a steady *crescendo* through the first two words, with 'loved' as the loudest point.

Also, I suggest that when words are repeated, they should be sung slightly more loudly the second time. This is because that's how we usually speak. One says, for example, 'Never, NEVER do that again.' So the second time the choir sing the words, 'God so loved the world' they should be stressed a little more firmly.

Then that phrase leads on to how God showed that he loved the world – 'that he gave his only begotten Son . . .'. The forward flow of the music and words is unstoppable – it goes right through to the wonderful words, 'everlasting life', which should be sung triumphantly. A similar unstoppable forward flow of music and words can be found in almost every section of Wesley's *Blessed be the God*.

You can find further examples of obvious and less obvious opportunities for creative word stress in almost every piece of music you conduct. Of course, you haven't time to point out every single example, so just highlight one or two examples at every rehearsal and you'll find your singers get really excited at this new way of singing.

I should point out, however, that there's one word in two famous pieces of music by Handel and Mozart, which you cannot help singing with incorrect syllabic stress – and that's the word '*Hal*-le-*lu*-jah!' (Hal-*le*-lu-*jah!*')

10. Singing with understanding

Once your choir is singing words really clearly and with proper stress, you need to address the matter of what the words mean.

(a) Not understanding the words

Not all singers understand what they're singing about. This is particularly true of children who have to be educated by you, week by week, into the basics of the Christian faith as they sing these incomparable texts. For example, I used to ask my new children to recite the Lord's Prayer from memory as one of the requirements to qualify to join my choir. Once they had done that successfully, I asked them what 'trespass' meant. Invariably they answered, 'Not going onto other people's property.' That's an obvious example of lack of understanding.

When I was rehearsing my arrangement of *Abide with me**
with my adult choir in America, someone asked why I had
put a picture of the Road to Emmaus on the cover. I had to
explain to them . . . Well, I'm sure you know why, don't you?

When you're singing hymns in a congregation, you'll
often find that your mind goes on auto-pilot; you'll sing
the most familiar hymn and realise afterwards that you've
no idea what you've been singing about. The same is
almost certainly true for members of your choir. It's up to
you to help them sing texts with their understanding as
well as with their well-trained voices.

It's also very easy the get the wrong message when
singing familiar words. For example, I asked my village
church choir recently, when they were rehearsing *Praise,
my soul, the King of heaven*, why the King of heaven should
praise my soul. One bass quickly saw the flaw in my question and explained the real meaning of that line. A line
which is often misunderstood is 'We shall see him, but in
heaven'. Another is, 'In pastures green, he leadeth me'.
Work those out for yourself.

Look at the first verse of Luther's hymn, *A mighty
fortress is our God*. Then look at the last line of that verse,
'On earth is not his equal'. Some singers may feel that they
could sing an optional 'Hallelujah' after that last line –
thanking God that he has no equal. But if you look more
carefully at the words of that verse, you'll find that that
last line does not refer to God at all. Quite the opposite.
There are many other examples in hymns and psalms
where the meaning is not always immediately apparent.

(b) Getting the message

Sometimes, when I'm listening to a choir singing hymns
or anthems, I get the feeling that they're concentrating on
getting the notes right, but have little idea of what the
message of the words is. What can be done about it?

(i) You – the choir director – have to understand what the
message of the words is and, what's more, you have to
care about that message. For instance, who was the man in
'Since by man came death'? And who was the man in 'By
man came also the resurrection of the dead'? (That's the
understanding part.) And then, am I aware in myself
about the consequences of sin ('death'), and have I experienced the resurrection life of Christ in my life?

That's strong meat. But let me go on. Am I excited
by the words of the music my choir sings, or am I just

* Published by Augsburg Fortress.

concerned with getting the notes right? It's the words that were the inspiration for the music, so let them inspire me and let them inspire my choir. The music is there to enable the message of the words to be more easily understood.

(ii) You – the choir director – must make that meaning clear to your singers. It's called doing your homework. It's called directing with authority. It's called spreading the Gospel. Once your singers really know what the words mean, then they can begin to convey that meaning through their singing – and this is not easy.

Many church choirs look so mournfully sincere that it's enough to put you off religion for life! Choristers should look pleasant when they're singing, but it's very hard to get one's choir to smile. I've seen a choir singing the first chorus in *Messiah* (And the glory of the Lord shall be revealed) looking as though they were reciting their thirteen times table in Greek! They looked so intense, without a spark of joy among any of them. So encourage your singers to look cheerful when they are singing about the Good News – this will not only help them to convey the joyful message of the words, but it will also help them to produce better tone. You cannot sing well when you're frowning. Try it.

And you have to encourage them every week to look cheerful, otherwise they'll slide further down that greasy pole.

So you need to address every one of these ten points at every rehearsal:

Right notes	Singing together
Breathing	Rhythm
Phrasing	Diction
Intonation	Word stress
Tone	Understanding

I'm suggesting that if you miss out any one of these at this week's rehearsal, the second law of thermodynamics will come into operation, and you'll find it twice as hard to correct that missed point next week.

And *always* do your homework, even for the 'easy' music. Failure to prepare is to prepare for failure.

CHAPTER 15

Create a positive 'Atmosphere'

There is such a thing as 'atmosphere' when you're leading a practice. By that I mean that when choirs habitually achieve much during their rehearsals, there's an atmosphere of on-going success and excitement from the very start. With choirs that don't achieve much, there's an atmosphere of boredom.

You can create a good atmosphere by leading your practices positively and energetically, in ways I've already suggested:

1. Achievement

For instance, by working on small details, so that your choir is continually making obvious progress; everything you ask them to do, they should ultimately be able to achieve – after three attempts! And your own attitude should be, 'I know that you can do it, and I'm really excited at the prospect of showing you how you can.'

2. Pace

You should lead your rehearsals in such a way that the forward flow of activity should carry everyone along together – rather like a surfer who is carried along by the crest of a wave, or a plane getting up the necessary speed to take off.

Whenever you stop the singing of your choir to make a point, make your constructive comment swiftly and in as few words as possible. Give your instructions so that your singers know exactly what you want – never theorise. So ask, 'Did you start together? Sing that first chord again. One, two, ready, breathe!'; 'Look at that expression mark and do something about it.' If your instructions take more than a couple of sentences, your singers' attention will begin to wane, and you will have lost that momentum, that atmosphere, which is essential to the leading of an excitingly creative rehearsal.

You shouldn't halt the practice by having a private conversation with a singer. You shouldn't have to stop and find out what the number of the next hymn is, or suddenly discover that an anthem hasn't been put out for rehearsal; because during those times the choir will have nothing to do – the wave of concentration and excitement will have collapsed and the surfer will have to wait, until another wave builds up.

So when you do your homework, plan your rehearsals in detail – know how long you will spend on warm-ups, how long you will rehearse hymns, how long you will rehearse next Sunday's anthem, how long you will spend looking at music for the following weeks.

I found it a great help, when leading my rehearsals in the USA, to write on the blackboard which was immediately behind the piano exactly what I was going to rehearse and in what order, including the numbers of the hymns and the pages in the anthem book, so that the singers could find their music before we began. That's a good way to begin creating the right atmosphere.

And always finish your rehearsals in an 'up-beat' manner, perhaps by enabling your choristers to sing several pages of music really well or, at the very least, to tell them, 'That was a great rehearsal. Thank you!' Always send them home happy.

3. Pastoral awareness

There's also a pastoral side to creating and sustaining a productive atmosphere. Recently I was leading a rehearsal with my small church choir and was asking each row of singers to sing a line of a hymn to see which row could sing it best. When I came to a row of three sopranos, they really made a mess of it, so I gave them a second chance. They still didn't do it nearly as well as the other singers, and so I said, 'They are trying hard, aren't they? Let's give them a clap.' And all the other singers burst into applause, relieving the tension. I heard afterwards that that round of applause meant a great deal to those ladies – 'We didn't get it right,' they said, 'but we did get a round of applause!'

A choir director must always be aware how the singers are feeling, because singing is such a personal way of making music. Nothing succeeds like success. If you begin your rehearsals efficiently, they will tend to continue efficiently, and create a good atmosphere from the start. But be sure to be aware when your singers need a break from their continuous concentration. Take a couple of minutes halfway through to relax the atmosphere with a few notices, so that they can sing even better for you in the second half of your demanding, good humoured and rewarding rehearsal.

4. Morale

Field-Marshal Montgomery said that the most important factor in all his successful campaigns was the morale of his troops. How is the morale of your choir?

CHAPTER 16

Warm-ups

The following practical ideas for warm-ups will work with both adults and children.

1. Get your singers to relax. They can't sing well if there's any tension in their bodies. Ask them to bounce up and down on their toes, then to shake their arms.

When they're standing still, they should roll their necks right round three times clockwise and three times anti-clockwise.

Then they should all sigh out to a long 'Ah', starting with a high *falsetto* and going down two octaves.

Some singers like to massage the neck and shoulders of the singer next to them, turning to the singer on their left, and then to the singer on their right. This can be great fun, as well as a very useful relaxing experience, if you have that sort of choir.

2. Get them breathing really well, knowing how to breathe deeply and low down, so that you may also encourage them to do this when they're singing anthems.

Say, 'Put one hand on your tummy (diaphragm) and the other on your side, so that you can feel expansion when breathing in, and contraction when breathing out.

'Sip in air as through a straw, while I count slowly up to four.

'Fill your whole body up with air, starting with your diaphragm. Keep your shoulders down, and make sure you are standing firmly on both feet.

'Hiss out, while I count slowly up to 10 – up to 12 – up to 15. Who managed to do that in one breath?'

3. Cultivate good tone. Sing each of these exercises in one breath, unaccompanied. Each exercise should be sung a semitone higher with each repetition. The choir will be able to do this without being asked, and without accompaniment, once you have indicated what they should do. The choir director should sing each exercise once, to show what is wanted, or else play the exercises clearly on the piano, and then have them sung unaccompanied. Always sing warm-ups unaccompanied, so that the singers can hear clearly what they are singing. Any accompaniment, however subtle, is bound to cover up some of their singing.

Feel two beats in a bar

Sing two repetitions to 'Ee' or 'Mmmee' (with rounded lips slightly forward), then up another semitone to 'Ah' or 'Mmmah' and stay on that vowel for the next three repetitions.

Encourage them to pull in their diaphragms to focus the upper notes more easily.

Continue to breathe deeply, keeping hands on tummy and side.

Feel four beats in a bar

Sing to 'Ee', then 'Eh' (which is more difficult – jaws should be dropped). Then sing to 'Aw' (with lips really pouting forwards) and finally 'Ah' (with jaw dropped low, and the back of the throat open).

Feel two beats in a bar

Sing this exercise to the same succession of vowels. When they sing *staccato* they should use their diaphragms to produce short notes, not their throats.

You'll need to encourage and challenge them every ten seconds or so to do better. Don't assume that they will sing their exercises well, however familiar these may be, unless you keep pushing them up that 'greasy pole'.

These three warm-up exercises may be sung progressively higher, as your singers (both adults and children) find through your vocal training that it is increasingly easy for them to sing high notes. Always start them on a D, but then, for subsequent exercises, you will find that they can, by easy stages, go up to an F, a G or even an A – sung, of course, to a clear 'Ah'.

Imagine yourself to be their sports coach – don't hide behind your piano, let them sing unaccompanied. Walk up and down among your singers so that you can look them straight in the eyes while they are singing their warm-ups. When you show such personal interest in them at such close quarters you will be challenging them to try even harder.

Seven easy stages to effective warm-ups

If your choir isn't accustomed to singing warm-ups and you aren't too sure of them yourself, try the following stages –

1. Basic minimum

Get your choir to sing unaccompanied the first chord of a hymn, such as *Praise, my soul*, to the vowel 'Ee'. Ask them to sing it fairly softly, and to sustain it for at least ten seconds while they listen to themselves and listen to each other.

This will help them to realise that they are not just a collection of individuals, but part of a composite whole. Also, by listening to each other they will tend to sing in tune and to sing with better balance.

While they are singing this and other music, call out to them occasionally, 'Well done, that's a lovely sound', and other encouraging words. If the singers know they're pleasing you, they'll try even harder for you.

But only hand out compliments if you really mean them. They can tell whether or not a compliment is deserved, so always be honest with your choir – but let all your comments be wrapped in kindness.

As I've said before, once you show that you're satisfied with what they are doing, they'll never do any better. So while the choir is singing say, 'Sopranos, listen to yourselves – are you really blending together? I can hear individual voices.' Or 'Tenors, sing that F sharp a fraction higher, please; listen to the other voices and you'll find out exactly where it should fit in.'

Make sure your singers' mouths are rounded – not stretched tight – with their lips pushed slightly forward. This will lead to more beautiful, resonant tone. Always keep on challenging your choir to sing better.

Then, having encouraged the choir to listen to themselves, you can start rehearsing the music for next Sunday.

2. Breathing exercises

After you and your choir have become more used to beginning practices with a simple warm-up, have them take a few deep breaths – with their hands on their diaphragms, so that they can feel that they are breathing correctly (see Chapter 8).

Then have your choir sing the first chords of several hymns to 'Ee' or 'Mmmee' as in stage one above.

3. Sustained notes

After a couple of weeks, add to the breathing exercises the singing of single sustained notes to a clear 'Ah', pitched around G. Say to them, 'Take a deep breath while I count up to four, then sing this note (play it now) to "Ah" while I count up to ten (one count per second).'

Afterwards, ask, 'How many of you managed to do that in one breath? Good! Now go up a semitone and sustain that note while I count to eleven . . .' And so on up to fifteen or even twenty.

You'll find that, once your singers are able to think, they'll be able to go up in semitones without you having to play the note for them. Gradually increase this over the next few weeks until you reach C above middle C, with the men singing an octave lower, of course.

Then go on to the singing of first chords of hymns, as before.

4. Downward scales

After doing the breathing exercise and singing sustained notes, add the singing of downward scales. Sing them unaccompanied to 'Ah', starting on C and gradually going up to the scale of E flat. Get your singers to sustain the last note for exactly four beats as you conduct them – coming off on the fifth beat. This will train them to follow your beat when you conduct anthems.

And don't forget to look at your singers while they are singing these warm-ups. You should walk up and down the rows of your choir, looking your singers straight in the face, individually and collectively, with an encouraging smile.

Continually encourage them to drop their jaws while singing 'Ah'. Many singers don't sing with really flexible jaws – so praise those singers who do, and encourage those who don't. They'll love you for it and sing so much better as a result.

5. Scales down and up

Have the choir sing their scales going down and coming up, in one breath, sustaining the final note for four beats. This requires super breath control, and it also means that they will be practising sustaining higher notes.

6. Scales in canon

Have them sing their scales in canon – with one side starting and the other side coming in two notes later. This will add a new dimension to their warm-ups and make them concentrate even more.

And once they've achieved singing in canon in two parts, try having them sing a scale in four-part canon – one row coming in after the other; or sopranos starting, then altos followed by tenors, and basses last. That will mean that those who start first will have to sustain their last note until everyone else finishes, and that will add to the challenges you are giving them.

7. Final exercises

Have them sing one or two of the exercises illustrated at the beginning of this chapter. Always finish with a two-octave scooped 'sigh' sung to 'Ah', beginning *falsetto* and going down as low as they can. This will ensure that they're thoroughly relaxed.

This is a very helpful exercise to encourage your adult singers to sing high notes with greater ease. (Sung firmly in unison to 'Ah', unaccompanied, but with the piano playing the interludes quietly to raise each repetition a semitone.)

Ah...   (Piano)   Ah...   (etc.)

Make sure (i) that they sing each exercise in one breath in strict time (some singers will breathe after the second note), (ii) that they **all** *crescendo* on the second note towards the third note, (iii) that the front of their mouths and the back of their throats are open – see page 73. Even the basses in my village church choir can sing top Gs easily when the exercise finally reaches F. Try it.

They'll love you for these warm-ups, and they'll love themselves too, because they'll feel they've achieved something worthwhile during the first few minutes of your rehearsal, and they'll look forward to achieving even more when you start practising hymns and anthems.

So you see – warm-ups aren't just for warming up the singers' voices, but for warming up their attitude to singing under your leadership.

CHAPTER 17

More tips about singing in tune

We have already noted that singing out of tune is an ongoing problem which needs constant correction (see Chapter 14, section 4). Here are some more thoughts on that topic.

Singing out of tune may be due to one or more of the following:

1. The singers are tired. Give them a couple of minutes' break in the middle of the rehearsal so that they can relax and recharge their batteries.

2. The singers are bored. It's up to you to inspire them.

3. The singers have been sitting down too long. They need to stand up to get their circulation going. Make sure that when they sit, they sit up straight. Bad posture automatically means bad vocal production. Instead of telling them to sit up straight, try saying, 'Show me how you should sit when you're singing.' You will find that they will immediately sit up straighter.

4. Your practice room may need some fresh air. Far too many choirs rehearse in ill-ventilated rooms. No wonder they sing out of tune, and no wonder they have trouble concentrating.

5. They're not producing their voices correctly. Show them how to do this (see Chapter 14, section 4).

6. No one has ever corrected them. This means that the cure is going to be especially difficult. The only way to deal with those singers who have a long-established problem and *always* sing out of tune is to spend a few minutes at every practice getting them to try to sing one note in tune; and then to sing just one short phrase in tune. Get them to sing softly and make sure that their posture is helpful. Over a period of time you will find that those singers will gradually improve.

7. The singers haven't been trained to listen to themselves, or to listen to what they are singing in relation to what the rest of the choir is singing (see Chapter 14, section 4).

8. They haven't been trained to listen to the chord given for an unaccompanied anthem. They may have heard it, but not really focused upon it with that meticulous precision which is needed for really singing in tune.

When you play the chord, play it only once – otherwise they won't really listen to it because they know you're going to play it again. Tell them you're going to play it only once – wait three seconds to make sure that everyone is listening, and then play it. You'll be surprised how much better they will sing for you right away.

9. Some music has built-in problems, which make it difficult to sing really in tune. Major thirds, perfect fifths and leading notes should always be tuned very slightly sharp. Your singers may not realise when these notes occur, but you should.

You can point out where a voice-part is singing the fifth of the chord – and ask them to sing it just a fraction higher. The tenors often have perfect fifths to sing, and the altos major thirds; while the sopranos often sing leading notes.

Another danger spot comes when a tune has several repeated notes. Singers subconsciously make less effort when they repeat a note; they think, 'I've already sung that note once, so it's bound to be OK when I sing it again.' And so, almost always, it flattens slightly. The same problem of 'I've already sung this' appears when singers return to a note that they've just sung.

The first two lines of *Once in royal David's city* are a good example of a tune which can easily lose pitch, because there are so many repeated notes as well as three leading notes. The second note is a leading note, and so it should be sung just a fraction sharp. The sets of repeated notes which follow can so easily drop in pitch.

The same problem arises in the short chorus, 'Since by man came death' from *Messiah*. In the last bar the altos and tenors have to return to a note they've already sung; for the altos it is a major third, and for the tenors a perfect fifth. Therefore those particular notes need, consciously, to be sharpened very slightly.

You can get your singers to sing just a fraction sharp in this case by starting your rehearsal of Handel's chorus with the final chord. Play it to them (when they're all listening) and get them to sing it absolutely in tune. Once they know how that final chord should sound, they will know where they should be aiming. Point out to the altos and tenors that their music needs special care in tuning.

You might get them to sing those last few notes in reverse order while playing their notes in sub-octaves on the piano. (This will help them to hear what you're playing while they're singing. They wouldn't be able to hear them as clearly if you played them in pitch.)

Then get them to sing the passage forwards – while still playing the notes in sub-octaves. Next, get them to sing without the piano, followed by the whole choir singing just that one bar very slowly while they are listening carefully to each other. As ever, do this at least twice, or even three times.

Sometimes it's helpful to ask your singers to sharpen the note immediately *before* a problem flat note. This applies here to the word 'came' – 'Since by man *came* death'.

Another time when singers find it difficult to sing in tune is when they are singing softly – then they tend to go flat. Soft singing is not lazy singing. It demands as much energy as loud singing. Choristers need to sing softly in a concentrated manner.

Ask them to whisper the words of the passage which should be sung softly. Tell them to whisper urgently. They'll find that they immediately make the consonants more precise and create a feeling of intensity about the whole approach.

Once they've experienced this intensity by whispering the words, get them to sing the words with the same feeling of focus. Then get them to sing it again, saying, 'It's better, but I still can't hear all the Ds.' Always give them one further specific thing to improve when you ask them to sing it again.

10. Some choir directors can't tell if their choir is in tune or not. They can't tell if they're sharp or flat and they don't know which voice-part is at fault, or which note begins the faulty intonation.

Singing out of tune always starts with one particular note. It may be a repeated note, or a note which is hard to pitch, or a note which the singers don't know how to sing easily because of faulty voice production. The director's job is to find that one note, isolate it, and get that particular voice-part to sing that single note really in tune. Once they know how it should sound, they can begin to sing it in context with more confidence.

You can learn to tell if a note is sharp or flat by 'doing your homework'. If you have played the music through on the piano several times, you will know how it should sound and so any faults, be they wrong notes or faulty intonation, will be more easy to spot. And you'll also know which singers need to correct them.

Sharp singing is more rare than singing flat, and it usually happens because the singers are over-excited. So let them relax for a few moments.

But whether sharp or flat, the method of correcting it should always be the same:

Define the problem.
Show them how that note should sound.
Get them to sing it – several times on their own.
Sing it in the context of a couple of bars.
Sing those bars with the rest of the choir.

Finally – always look encouraging, never pained or stressful when correcting faults. If you look stressed, your choir will feel stressed. The correcting of details should always be seen as something which can be achieved with the right encouragement. So always be encouraging, even when they fail.

CHAPTER 18

Some more advanced techniques

1. Where is the tune?

In some anthems the melody isn't always sung by the sopranos; it may be sung by the altos or the tenors, or even the basses. Not all conductors are fully aware of where the melody is in such cases, because they haven't done their homework. Sometimes it may be for only a few bars, and sometimes for a whole page. One example where the melody is in the soprano line for only a very few bars indeed is Duruflé's setting of *Ubi Caritas*. Not all conductors realise this.

The conductor needs to point out to the singers where the melody is, and to ask that particular voice-part to sing it just a little bit more firmly while the other voices sing a little bit more softly. And they should all listen to each other so that every singer can hear the tune wherever it happens to be.

2. The music must never stop, even in rests

This is a point which even some illustrious choir directors miss; and it has to do with the sense of forward movement which music must have if it is to live. Some conductors have a blind spot when it comes to conducting songs which have separate verses. They seem to feel that the music stops at the end of each verse, and so nothing happens between the stanzas.

What they *should* feel is a sense of rhythm in the silences between each verse. The singing of hymns in church is a good example of what I mean. It's helpful to give exactly two beats' rest in between each verse.

There are organists who hang on to the last chord of verses for an extra two or three beats after the singers have stopped. This kills all sense of rhythmic flow. Some organists who know what they ought to do have a real problem in taking their hands off the keys rhythmically. It's the 'click' of silence which gives a forward impetus to enable singers to feel two beats' clear rest before they begin the next verse.

Je - sus Christ her lit - tle__ child__(d). *(breathe!)* He came

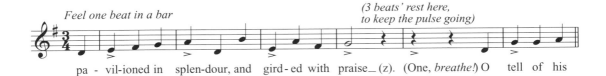

Feel one beat in a bar

(3 beats' rest here, to keep the pulse going)

pa - vil-ioned in splen-dour, and gird-ed with praise_ (z). (One, *breathe!*) O tell of his

That's what conductors should do when they're leading folk song arrangements which have gaps between verses. It needn't always be two beats' rest – it all depends on the music itself – but there should be a definite sense of rhythmic flow from the very first note of the song right through to the end of the last chord.

It's the same when choirs sing psalms to Anglican chants. Many choirs tend to stop, not only between verses but also at the halfway point in the middle of verses, instead of feeling, in those brief silences, that essential sense of forward movement which will enable the flow to lead the words and the music on. Music which stops, which comes to a standstill, has died, and some choral conductors don't realise this. One helpful way to encourage this sense of forward flow during choral rests in psalms is to have the organist accompany with continuous sound – no breaks at all between verses and half verses.

I'm not saying that choirs should ignore rests in the music. But I am saying that whether there are rests, or whether there are gaps between stanzas of a song or verses of a psalm, the singers need to feel a sense of forward movement – otherwise the music dies. Those who have the precious gift of musicianship will know what I'm talking about, but those who don't, alas, won't.

3. The ability to create long phrases

Most choral conductors are able to train their choirs to sing in short phrases (although I've known quite a few who can't), but very few choir directors can inspire their singers to create a really long line musically.

This is because they're so intent on getting their choirs to sing the right notes, and to sing them loudly or softly, and to get them to enunciate clearly, that they have no time to think of the essential grace of music – which is the creation of beautiful long phrases.

In other words, they are so intent on thinking in terms of what the music is doing right now, that they don't think about what it will be doing through the next two or three pages. The music must rise and fall in lovely lines as a long-term concept, and it is the breath which gives life both to a body and also to music.

Howells' *Requiem* is a very good example of what I mean. There's a movement in that work which calls for a continuous *crescendo*, lasting for nearly three pages. It's incredibly exciting to sing and also to conduct, when the singers and conductor can visualise the growth of the music so far ahead.

It's rather like going for a walk in the country and seeing before you the top of a hill half a mile away. You can see it getting nearer as you walk towards it, but your eyes must be lifted up as you walk, not looking down to the ground, i.e. not thinking about individual notes, but being able to see the whole picture.

There are other pieces which give similar opportunities for long phrases, such as the first couple of pages of S. S. Wesley's *Blessed be the God and Father* (although the first page has no *crescendo*, but it must have a sense of forward movement), and Stanford's *Nunc Dimittis* in B flat (where the *crescendos* are clearly sectional).

Beware, when your choir is singing soft music, that they don't make it sound dull. Some choirs, when they sing softly, seem to sing with a somewhat negative feeling. This is often noticeable in interpretations of the first page of Wesley's *Blessed be the God*, which should be sung with a sense of repressed excitement. Look at the meaning of those amazing words: 'God . . . hath begotten us again unto a lively hope by the resurrection of Jesus Christ from the dead.'

Similarly, when some choirs sing the opening pages of Howells' *Collegium Regale Magnificat*, they seem to be so intent upon singing those words softly, with approximately the right rhythm, that they do not catch the essential spirit of delicate joy of the text: 'My soul doth magnify the Lord . . .'. (You can hear, on a CD, how it was sung by the choir for which it was written: Boris Ord: the Choir of King's College, Cambridge. Testament SBT 1121.)

You can find other examples of music which have long phrases in some of Bruckner's choral works. It's up to the choir director to realise where they are, and to inspire his or her singers to recreate long flows of inexpressible beauty. It calls for a tremendous amount of self-control, as well as creative musical imagination, to bring it off, but it's so wonderfully worthwhile, and the effect on an audience is stunning.

4. Time signatures

Not all choral conductors really look at the time signature of the work they are conducting, or the directions for changes of tempo.

For example, I know of only one choir director who conducts Stanford's B flat *Nunc Dimittis* in minims. Stanford wrote a 2/2 signature, but every other choir director I've seen conducts it in 4/4, which makes it much too slow – thus making the long-drawn-out climax, written in minims, impossible to sing. Once conductors realise that this miniature classic has to be felt in minim beats rather than crotchet beats, its whole character changes – it's faster and even joyful, instead of slow and turgid.

Hymns are often sung with a relentless four beats per bar: '*On-ward! Christ-ian sold-iers*' – when they would sound much better and move more easily and the meaning of the words would come through more clearly if they were sung with two beats per bar: '*On*-ward! *Christ*-ian *sold*-iers.'

Organists can help the choir and congregation feel music in 2/2 – or even 1/1 – time, by amending their touch. For example, instead of playing four heavy beats in a bar (as I heard one organist do recently):

try lightening your touch so that you feel only two beats, or even one steady beat, per bar:

Feel two beats in a bar

This is such an important point, for it applies not only to hymns but to almost every other piece of music your choir sings. The fewer beats there are per bar (for example, beating minims instead of crotchets) the more musical the notes will sound.

Hymns which are in 3-time should be felt as one beat per bar, to help them flow more easily: 'The *day* thou *gav*-est, *Lord*, is *end*-ed.'

5. Controlling *diminuendos* and *crescendos*

Diminuendos

When there's a *diminuendo* at the end of a phrase, I often ask my choirs to *diminuendo* to silence. Many choirs, when they're making a *diminuendo*, get softer to about halfway through the note or phrase, and then they seem to reach a plateau of softness and don't get any quieter. It's a most beautiful effect if a choir can so control its *diminuendos* that the sound disappears at exactly the right time.

That means, of course, that they have to sustain the note for its full written length. If a final note is four beats long, and if it's followed by a rest, the silence should begin exactly at the start of the rest.

Some choirs tend to think of *diminuendos* as concave in shape, rather than convex. In other words choirs need to begin to get softer more slowly, or keep louder longer, instead of sounding like a pricked balloon. Once they can do that there's still plenty of sound left from the halfway point to enable them to go on getting softer; and it's the matter of going on going on getting softer which is the secret of a really well-controlled *diminuendo*.

Diminuendos should be sung with a sense of forward movement. Few choral directors seem to realise this, for they tend to make their choirs' *diminuendos* sound like a retreat instead of a beautiful musical experience. If they are perceived as going backwards they will collapse far too quickly. Instead, visualise *diminuendos* as going forwards – you'll notice the difference immediately.

By the way, very few choirs can sing really softly. When a passage is marked *p*, many singers sing *mf*. There's nothing quite so magical as a choir which can sing *pianissimo*. I commend you to ask your choir to sustain one chord for ten seconds, first *mezzo forte*, then for another ten seconds *piano*, then *pianissimo*, and then *ppp*! (Make sure that they all start to sing together, rhythmically, for it's so easy for a choir to think that singing softly means singing lazily.) Once they experience this, they will have a wonderful new palette of colour to add to their growing technique.

Crescendos

Crescendos need to go on going on getting louder. Some choirs seem to make a *crescendo* at the beginning of a note or phrase, but aren't able to keep it going, because they get too loud too soon. So get your choir to start their *crescendos* relatively softly.

The danger in singing *crescendos* is that some singers may be tempted to force their tone and make a nasty noise – and sometimes go sharp. Basically, a choir should not change tone for *crescendos* or *diminuendos*. The sound should just get gradually louder or softer, without getting rough or anaemic, respectively.

Also, when an anthem finishes with a loud chord, the choir should continue to give it a sense of forward movement by making a slight *crescendo*, rather than feel that it stops. This will give that final chord a wonderful sense of life. Do this even if the chord is marked *fortissimo* – just don't make the *fortissimo* so loud that it can't get any louder. Singers should always have something in reserve, be it breath or volume.

6. Being able to bend the pulse

A director should be able to conduct his or her choir in such a manner that, at the end of a phrase, the choir may take a relaxed breath before starting the next phrase. It often happens that when singers reach the end of a phrase, they find it very difficult to have enough time to breathe without snatching it, and therefore they make the previous syllable too loud.

To deal with this, directors need to be able to hear in their heads exactly what it is that they want, so that they can instruct their choirs clearly. The director needs to slow the pulse imperceptibly just before they breathe, then they take their breath without any feeling of hurry or tension, and start the next phrase immediately up to tempo (otherwise they will sing slower and slower).

To avoid doing this, by adding half a beat or so to the measure, requires careful preparation of the choir by the conductor. But you *can* get your choir to carry out this so-called advanced manoeuvre, first by telling them what they are about to do, and secondly getting them to do it with your help. And it does depend entirely on how the director conducts. You must conduct in a very relaxed manner, with loose, flexible wrists. If you show the slightest trace of tension, it won't work!

There's a good example of this in Stainer's *God so loved the world*, at the top of the second page where the choir sings loudly the chord of D major to the word 'life'. The challenge is to sing the following soft chord really accurately, after having sung the loud one, and so a good conductor will realise that the singers need just a little more time to 'change gear' – to focus not only on the next note, but also to be able to sing it with confident accuracy and musicianship.

I'm always looking ahead, and so I conduct 'life' with three firm beats and a slight *crescendo*, to make that chord live; but then I bring them off gently, so that they can feel a 'soft' rest – and I extend that single rest to make it just a little bit longer, to enable the singers to focus really confidently on their next note. Keep your hands moving slowly when you conduct that slightly stretched one-beat rest, otherwise the forward movement will stop.

By the way, many choirs get softer on 'life' because they're running out of breath. It's important that that chord be held for its full three beats really loudly, even making a slight *crescendo* on it, for it is the climax of that wonderful verse in St. John's Gospel.

Some choral conductors bring off their singers on final chords as though they were trying to get rid of a tarantula they've picked up. Others bounce their hands several times as though they were about to serve at tennis. (As the conductor's hands are bouncing so much, the choir could well ask, 'Where's the beat?') Yet others stand with their arms rigidly outstretched as though they've seen a vision. No – your choir needs to know exactly how long that final chord will last, so bring them off with a flowing movement of the arm, relaxed wrist and hand. This musical gesture should mirror the mood of the music: a gentle gesture for gentle music, and a more precise movement for louder music. Better still, continue beating time with your right hand during a final chord, so that your singers can count the beats, while your left hand is raised to show that that chord is being sustained. Let your choir see, physically, where the chord will finish as your arm moves expressively. The secret of achieving neat endings is to indicate the beat immediately before you bring them off (. . . *and*, off!).

7. Conducting relaxed breathing

If you want your choir to take a relaxed breath, how should you conduct? Should you be relaxed or should you be extraordinarily precise? The right answer is to be relaxed.

Not many conductors know that. They have no conception of conducting in the mood of the piece. If the mood is calm, you must convey calmness by your gestures. If it's energetic, you need to conduct energetically (but not flamboyantly). And so when the time comes to take a breath, conductors need slightly to slow the tempo in a relaxed manner, and move their forearm and hand so that the choir can actually see, physically, where the next beat will start. The choir can then work out for themselves exactly where to breathe, especially if the conductor breathes with them.

Here's another good example from Stainer's *God so loved the world* – measure 28 – where the choir has to breathe together and then start the new phrase, and there are no rests there to help them. They have to add almost an extra half-beat's rest in order to sing that measure without any feeling of rush.

Written:

world to   con - demn the world, God   sent not   his

Sung with relaxed tempo in 2nd bar: *(a tempo)*

world to   con - demn the world,   God   sent not   his

Sir David Willcocks' arrangement of *Away in a manger** has a lot of running quavers in it. That Christmas carol must be sung in a relaxed manner, but the difficulty lies in some of the inner voices which have to take a breath at the ends of phrases when they're supposed to be singing continuous quavers.

I mark exactly where the choir should breathe (and it's at almost every punctuation mark) and we have to practise doing it, first by taking too much time to breathe, and then doing it again while we try to keep the music flowing

* In *Carols for Choirs 1* (Novello)

inevitably forward – which I encourage by conducting a fluid three beats in a measure, 'bending' the pulse when breaths are taken.

I find that if I indicate where the breaths should come by raising my entire arm, from the elbow, that gives the choir sufficient notice of where and how they should breathe. They're able to 'bend the time' without actually feeling that the pulse has stopped.

There's a similar moment in Stanford's *Beati quorum*, three pages from the end, when the choir needs a fraction of a second longer to breathe easily, before starting the next phrase gently: '. . . *integra est*, (relaxed breath, even though there's no rest) *quorum via* . . .'. It will work if you encourage your choir to relax at this point and to watch you, singing those few notes from memory.

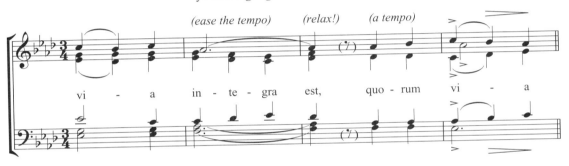

If the conductor can feel the pulse moving forward, then the choir will too.

8. Expressive rests

There's another thing that I learned recently about conducting rests. Look at the end of Parry's anthem, *Lord, let me know mine end*:

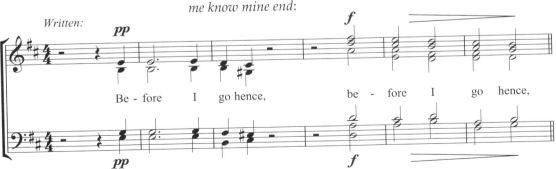

Here we have the opposite of the Stainer anthem above. The choir ends one phrase softly and starts the next one loudly, instead of vice versa.

It's very difficult indeed to achieve this successfully. The choir needs to be able to finish the first phrase quietly without being distracted from what's coming next. Fortunately Parry put four beats' rest here before the choir has to sing the next entry loudly, and so I conduct the first two beats' rest softly, and then the next two beats' rest very loudly, to enable the singers to come in on the next chord really firmly.

Rests – really expressive rests – are as important as really expressive notes.

9. Singing into the echo

If you are fortunate enough to conduct your choir in a church or cathedral which has a long reverberation period, use every opportunity to make use of that echo. One of the most exciting musical experiences you can create is to get your choir to 'sing into the echo'. Such opportunities occur when one phrase ends loudly, and the next one begins quietly, such as in Stainer's much-quoted anthem, *God so loved the world* – top of page 2: '. . . everlasting life. For God sent . . .'. If your choir can sing 'For God sent . . .' more softly than the sound of the continuing echo which resulted from its *forte* singing of 'life', you will have created a moment of magic.

The classic example of this occurs in the opening pages of E. W. Naylor's eight-part anthem, *Vox dicentis*, when the choir sings very loudly, '*Quid, quid clamabo?*' ('What shall I cry?'). The next very soft phrase, '*Omnes caro*' ('All flesh is grass') sounds wholly mystical when it emerges through the echo.

10. Bringing out interesting polyphonic melodies

This is a subtle point that I learnt from Dr Boris Ord when I studied with him at Cambridge. It applies when you're conducting a polyphonic anthem which has interesting melodies in all the voice parts.

Dr Ord focused the attention of the listeners onto the voice part that was about to sing an interesting phrase, however short or long it might be, by getting those voices to make a slight crescendo a couple of beats before their melody began.

Discover the places in your polyphonic anthems where the tenors or the altos or even the basses have a short melody which is worth hearing, and write in a little crescendo a couple of beats before their tune starts. (Generally, the interesting lines come where the notes are blackest.)

In that way, the attention of the audience will switch easily from one voice-part to another, and that leads to really creative listening, which comes from really creative rehearsing, which comes in its turn from really creative preparation.

11. Music by Herbert Howells

Frequently, in Howells' music, he ties a quaver to the end of a long note:

He did this, not to add an extra half beat to that long note, but to ensure that the long note was sustained for its full length. Here, for example, 'God' should be sung for exactly four beats, with the 'd' sung at the start of the fifth beat. The reason for this slightly awkward-looking system of notation is that many choirs, when Howells was a young man, tended to cut short final notes. (This is still practised by many leading choirs today.)

Howells did *not* intend 'God' to be sung for four and one half beats, as some conductors mistakenly believe (putting the 'd' at the start of the second half of a beat, which you can only do successfully if you are prone to hiccups).

I knew Dr Howells and asked him about this specific point. He told me that he had got into the habit of tying quavers at the end of long notes and did it almost automatically. The trouble is that he was not always consistent. So ensure that Howells' long notes are sung musically and not awkwardly. His long notes and long phrases should invariably be sung with a sense of forward movement and with steady, almost imperceptible *crescendos* towards important syllables. His music was created to be sung in graceful 'curves', with tremendous breath control, and never in straight lines.

12. Young choir directors

Young choir directors sometimes conduct meditative music too slowly. They do this in order to bring out the beauty of the music and the meaning of the words (which are admirable aims). However, they tend to forget that music must have a live heart-beat; the pulse must enable the music to flow forwards and 'fly', much as an aeroplane must move at a certain minimum speed, otherwise it will fall out of the sky.

This tendency to conduct music too slowly is particularly true when you are recording or broadcasting. Slow-moving music needs to be sung just a little bit faster when an audience cannot see you.

Some young choir directors also tend to ask their choirs to over-phrase, i.e. to make final soft syllables too soft. So ask yourself, young musician, if you can hear clearly the final syllables of words such as 'Saviour', 'blessed', 'generations'. Similarly, ask yourself if you slow down too much at the end of hymns and anthems. They're not the end of Wagner's *Ring*!

So, young conductors, I commend your musicianship, but suggest that you should beware of musical introspection. I used to fall into these traps myself when young, but grew out of them!

Three final conducting tips

1. If you really want to control the singing of your choir you should stand as near to them as possible. The nearer you are to your singers, the more impact and creative communication there will be between you and your choir.

If the choir are singing with an orchestra, it will not be possible for you to stand near them – and so you'll have to rehearse them at a distance so they can get used to it. But, at rehearsal, try standing near them and then standing further away – and you'll see that being near your singers really does help you to control them more easily, as long as you remember to look at them and not at your music.

2. If you want your choir to sing with rich tone, try conducting low down, on the level of your diaphragm. This will tend, subconsciously, to encourage them to sing with chest tone. If, on the other hand, you want a lighter tone, conduct with your hands held higher, around your head.

3. One of the most exciting experiences a conductor and his or her choir can have is to sing at a concert even more wonderfully than they did at their finest rehearsal. How can you achieve this?

(a) Build up the 'sense of occasion' for the performance, giving your choir an inspired 'pep talk' immediately before you go on to the platform (see Chapter 21).

(b) But before that, conduct every rehearsal so that you hold your singers in the palms of your hands – so that making even the slightest movement with your hands always produces the musical result you want. In other words, conduct so creatively that you can actually feel yourself 'playing' your choir – in a similar manner to a pianist playing his instrument. If you have the slightest feeling that you are fighting your choir, or for ever urging them on because they're not really responding, this is something which you will have to work at (see Chapter 6).

(c) But above all, you must have a passionate love for the music you are conducting and know everything about it, and you must have an equally strong commitment to all your singers, both individually and collectively.

It's a prize worth striving for.

By the way, when your choir is singing with an orchestra the singers will generally be placed behind the players. This will mean that they will tend to sing fractionally behind your beat. Therefore, in your rehearsals and especially the dress rehearsal, you should (i) tell them about this tendency, so that they may continually take responsibility themselves for singing with surer attacks, and (ii) galvanise them with compelling eye contact and with mouthing of the words throughout the performance to encourage them to sing with focused precision. Also, in the softer passages the choir may tend to sing slightly flat, so prepare them to do something about that, too.

CHAPTER 19

Some hints for organists

Playing hymns

When leading hymns, the organist's major role is to encourage the singing of the congregation – by helping them to begin together, maintaining a good pace and setting a mood to match the hymn being sung.

1. Leading in and maintaining the pace

A very good way to get the congregation to come in more surely than they sometimes do is to play the first chord rather detached, instead of playing it *legato*. A small break between the first and second chords will 'jump start' the congregation by giving them a firm sense of rhythm to follow –

You can keep that sense of rhythm going by continuing to play the right hand and some off-beat pedal notes rather detached and filling in *legato* notes or chords in the left hand –

2. Setting the mood

Sometimes organists swamp the singing of the congregation by playing hymns too loudly. They don't always realise how loudly they are playing as they continue with relentlessly unyielding sounds for a whole verse (or even a whole hymn).

Therefore, try starting fairly loudly, and then gradually reduce the sound during the second line of the hymn, while maintaining the same colour. You could do this by taking off a Great mixture and gradually closing the Swell box. That should be more than enough sound to support, but not drown, the congregation.

I heard Sir John Dykes Bower do this in St Paul's Cathedral many years ago. He was able to support the singing of a congregation of several thousand using this method. He reduced the volume of the organ from *ff* to *mf* quite quickly. It was an object lesson on how it could be done.

Playing anthems

1. Playing anthem interludes

When you are accompanying an anthem and you come to an interlude for organ only, let it be played slightly louder than the previous accompanimental passage. This is because the addition of a few stops, or the changing from Swell to Great for those few bars, will help to carry the momentum of the music forward. The essence of those few solo bars for organ is that the musical focus moves from the singers to the organ which, previously, had been in a supportive, rather than a solo role.

2. Peeling off chords

It is helpful, especially if your church has only a little resonance, to 'peel off' final chords of pieces, starting with the top notes in the right hand, through the left hand and ending with the feet.

Think of it as playing a broken chord in reverse. Instead of starting with the playing of the bottom note first and quickly adding notes above – thus making a broken chord – you do the opposite: you release the top note, then the note below that, and so on, until you are left with just the pedal note sounding.

If done too slowly it would sound a bit Victorian, but not if it's done in a split second – so fast that it's not really noticeable. It takes the unwanted 'click' out of what should be a rounded final chord. This is particularly helpful when the final note includes a solo played on a reed stop. Release that solo stop a fraction of a second before the accompaniment, for reed stops certainly have a 'click' when they are released.

Releasing your final chord at the end of an anthem a split second before the choir finishes is also a very practical technique to cultivate. This is because the organ sound always seems to linger a fraction of a second after the organist takes his or her hands off the keys.

It's the same when the organist is playing with an orchestra. Take your hands and feet off the final chord half a second before the orchestra stops playing – especially if that final chord is a loud one. The effect will be that you've all stopped playing together.

Registering romantic organ music

When you are playing Romantic organ music, especially music by British composers such as Stanford or Howells, you need to change your registration, subtly, every four bars or so. This is particularly true when playing soft, expressive passages. For example, for a piece which starts softly on the Swell, use 8ft flute and 8ft string (not Celeste), than add 4ft flute for the next phrase; then take off the string, leaving you with 8 and 4 flutes. Add 8ft Diapason when it gets a little louder. Be sparing in the use of high mixtures, and use Celestes for a very few bars only, at really emotional moments.

When the final few bars are played on Celestes, it can be very effective to take off the Celestes for the last chord – leaving the Gamba on its own – while you make an exquisite *diminuendo* by closing the box very slowly.

When playing louder music, be lavish in your subtle use of the Swell box, and always add Swell stops with the box closed, so that you can make a *crescendo* through the next phrase. In other words, think orchestrally. Insert a solo for the Clarinet or Oboe when the opportunity arises. When playing on the Swell, look out for lower parts in the left hand which could be soloed out, subtly, on the Great.

Frequently in accompaniments, and also organ solos, there are interesting melodies, or short phrases, written in the tenor register. These cannot clearly be heard when both hands are playing on the same manual. (Listen to see if you can hear these tenor notes.) Therefore try soloing them out, subtly, when your right hand is on the Swell, with your left hand playing on the Great 8ft flute, coupled to the Swell, or even an occasional Clarinet solo. Let your accompaniments continually change colour to enhance the beauty of the music. A beautiful example of a brief solo left-hand melody can be found in the 4th bar of Brahms' *How lovely are thy dwellings fair* – immediately before the choir enters for the first time. A similar moment (with a triplet figure added) can be found when this opening is repeated towards the end.

I say all this because I was taught the organ by a pupil of Stanford – Dr Harold Darke – who was also a close friend of Howells. Some organists seem to tend to play Romantic organ music as though they were registering Bach, i.e. several pages on one set of stops. No – when you have played one four-bar phrase on one registration, the next four-bar phrase should almost always be played with a slightly different colour.

What I am saying is that you should be colourfully creative in your registration for Romantic organ music. And not only then, but also when you accompany anthems, hymns and psalms.

CHAPTER 20
Playing right notes confidently and musically

If you have difficulty in playing the right notes on the organ or piano on Sunday or for a recital, there's a very simple solution. All you have to do is to practise the right notes and not the wrong ones. This is so obvious, but very few players, especially children, actually do it. The secret lies in practising so slowly that you *know* that the next note or chord *will* be right. I've said it before: there's no such thing as a difficult note. The difficulty lies in *getting to* that note. One's mind is rather like a computer. You get out of it what you put in. If you feed in right notes, then right notes will the more surely come out.

It takes an enormous amount of self-control to do this really effectively. You have to work out the fingering of the passage first. If you normally ignore the fingering and just use the next available finger that comes along, you are almost certain to make mistakes. I suggest that you can only play with assured accuracy when you have worked out which fingers will play which notes. The whole idea of practising is to make the piece easier for you. If the notes aren't getting easier as you practise, you aren't practising it properly.

If there are difficult places in the music where you *know* that you're going to play the wrong notes, the reason is because you are actually *practising* playing the wrong notes. It's so very simple. Think about it!

You see, when you are practising music, you are not only practising playing the notes, you're also practising your state of mind. If you tend to play wrong notes when a difficult passage comes up, that means that you are worrying about playing wrong notes, and therefore you are actually practising worrying.

To avoid this, I practise four bars at a time, very slowly indeed – one note every two seconds – however fast the notes should be. Thus I *know* that the next note will be right; I can actually feel it in my fingers before I play it. Playing as slowly as that dissolves all need to worry, and so I find that I'm actually practising feeling relaxed and happy about playing those so-called difficult notes.

I play those four bars absolutely correctly three times in succession. If I do make a mistake I start all over again, which means that I play the notes even more slowly.

If you think that you will be wasting time practising right notes like that, I suggest that you are actually wasting more time practising the wrong ones – which is what we all do when we practise too fast. *And* we also practise getting worried and tense.

I play those four bars, keeping relaxed, but also keeping my mind concentrated, enjoying every note, with no worries or tension. I then play them three times in a different rhythm: instead of playing steady crotchets, for example, I turn them into dotted-crotchet quaver. Or if most of the notes are quavers, I turn them into dotted-quaver semiquaver.

Then I do the reverse rhythm: quaver dotted-crotchet, or whatever.

This means that I will then have played those four bars nine times in succession absolutely correctly. And then I go on to the next four bars.

I always play slowly enough to *know* that the next note will be right, so that I can practise feeling calm and actually enjoy the music – for that is what it's all about, isn't it? You see, when I give my recital I want to feel wholly confident – which means practising being wholly confident by playing really slowly when I first learn a piece.

It is such a joy to *know* that you will play right notes, for that means that you can then concentrate upon interpreting the music rather than worrying about the mechanics of playing notes.

Fugue in G minor, J. S. Bach. BWV 542

It's very simple to say, but very difficult to do, because one finds that one begins to speed up without meaning to. That's why I discipline myself to play short passages three times right consecutively. Playing them three times right and three times wrong won't work; wrong information is being fed into one's mind.

And playing hands and feet separately is good too. Anything you can do to make the piece really easy for yourself is most certainly well worth doing. Only when the notes are really secure can you begin to play a little faster, but never stray outside the boundary of *knowing* that the next note will be wholly secure.

But the matter of getting the notes right is only the first stage in learning a piece of music. Once the notes are secure you can then begin to pay more attention to what the notes are saying. In other words, the mechanics of playing notes are to enable you to begin to create music.

Howells and Messiaen often wrote a text at the start of their organ music. Is that text coming alive by my playing? Reubke wrote his major organ work on words from the ninety-fourth Psalm. Have I taken the trouble to discover which sections of the music were inspired by individual verses? If not, then I am not fully realising Reubke's intentions, and my interpretation will be the less meaningful.

Bach's Chorale Preludes and Partitas for organ were composed not only to explore the beauty of the chorale melodies, but also especially to bring out the meaning of the text of the hymns for which those tunes were written. In order to understand why Bach wrote what he did, it's very helpful to write the words of the hymns over the elaborated *cantus firmus*. Then you will understand, for example, why the end of *O Mensch, bewein* ('O man, thy grievous sin bewail') is to be played very slowly – because Christ was on his Cross for a *long* time ('. . . Kreuze lange'). And, once you understand that Bach portrayed the varying moods of each line of the text in his music, you can even impute joy to the line, 'The dead he raised to life again.'*

Do I really listen to the sounds that the organ makes when I am playing, or is my attention only on the mechanics of playing with skilful fingers and feet? All organs and all churches and concert halls are different; therefore the way we play our music on one organ will not be wholly appropriate when we play it elsewhere.

For example, Blackburn Cathedral has a reverberation of more than six seconds. During my 18 years as director of music there we welcomed many guest recitalists, but

---

* Full texts of the chorales can be found in Books 15 and 20 of the Novello edition of Bach's organ works. Also, see Peter Williams' *The Organ Works of Bach*, volume 2, Cambridge University Press, which is currently being reprinted. Hermann Keller's book, with the same title (Peters), is also an invaluable source of illuminating information.

less than half a dozen of them realised that our organ required a special technique if all the notes were to be heard clearly. The best of these was Daniel Chorzempa, a young American organist who lived in Cologne. When he played I could hear every note – even running semi-quavers – with crystal clarity. And instead of looking at his hands when he was playing, he looked at the organ pipes, which were some way from the console.

After his recital I asked him how he had achieved such musical clarity. He gave me a devastating two-word answer: 'I listen!'

Very few organists really listen to the sounds they are creating – whether it be playing hymns, accompanying anthems or giving recitals. Some performers play the notes; others play the music. Some achieve the first through assiduous practice, but only a very few achieve the second by always listening critically to themselves with musical sensitivity.

CHAPTER 21

More practical tips

Rehearse in service conditions

If, despite your enlightened teaching, you find that your choristers still don't sing as well on Sundays as they did on Fridays, it may be because they haven't rehearsed in church. It's important to rehearse in service or concert formation, for each singer needs to feel what it's like to sing with his or her neighbour.

If the configuration of the singers in your practice room is different from their position in church, you ought to think about altering the way your seats are placed for rehearsals. As you are rehearsing the music for Sunday's service, you need also to rehearse in the configuration which the singers will experience in church.

I hadn't realised how much difference it made to the actual sound of a choir until I experimented with different placings of my Princeton Singers. The moving of just one singer from the back row to the front row made a noticeable difference to the balance of the voices. And so, as you want your choir to sound well balanced on Sunday, they need to stand in that configuration when they rehearse.

Conducting from the console

I disagree strongly with musicians who conduct from the console, even though some music colleges actually run courses on how to do it. I disagree because I train my choirs to be self-sufficient; I train them to make the choir director dispensable. If they can only sing well when I'm standing in front of them, then I'm not doing my job properly.

When I'd been at my cathedral in England for only a few weeks, one of the tenors came to see me and said, 'You will be leading us from the organ, won't you?' I said, 'No, I shall be *accompanying* you.' He didn't know what to make of that, because my distinguished predecessor had always led the choir from the console. It took them a long time to get used to our reversed roles.

Not conducting from the console

I trained my adult choirs and also my younger singers in England and America to be self-reliant – and they were all local amateurs; we're not necessarily talking about trained professionals. They were all responsible enough to know how to stand up together – to concentrate their attention on the leaders* sitting on either side of the stalls, who would give the signal to stand. These leaders also gave the signal when to breathe for the start of the accompanied anthem, and I watched from the organ console for them to give the final cut-offs. They made *crescendos* and *diminuendos* themselves, without having their conductor throw himself into contortions, because I gave the responsibility to them at my practices to do all these things. So they became thinking choirs; and I'm doing the same now, step by step, with my small church choir in the depths of the Lancashire countryside.

And the whole point of having a choir which is trained to conduct itself for accompanied anthems means that they will try harder than if you were to conduct them, and therefore they will sing better. Some music colleges these days teach students how to conduct their choirs, but they don't teach them how to train their choirs to be able to conduct themselves – and it's so rewarding to do, for it eventually produces much better results.

Asking questions

I've always encouraged my choirs to think for themselves by asking them questions (see Chapters 9 and 10). You can use this effective technique with choirs of all sizes, though obviously you can ask more questions of a church or school choir than you can of a choral society.

Nevertheless, I suggest that you should still encourage the members of your large choral society to think for themselves. Instead of telling them to sing softly, or more loudly, say, for example, 'Please look at that expression mark and do what it says.' Then, as ever, you will need to get them to do it at least twice more before you are satisfied; and so you might say, 'Some of you are still not doing what that expression mark tells you to. Let's try it again.' And then, for the third time, say with a smile, 'There might be one or two of you who don't quite realise what *piano* means. So, will everyone tell his or her neighbour what it means, and then we'll have one more attempt.'

This is simply another way of asking a question, which makes every individual singer work out the answer for themselves. By throwing the responsibility onto your singers like this you will get them to sing better than if you'd just told them to sing softly and then got cross with

* For more about choir leaders and standing and sitting, see 'Standing and sitting', page 120.

them for not doing it. Having thought it out for themselves they will take pride in singing it really softly in the concert.

No choir really sings willingly if the conductor browbeats them. I have heard of some conductors who do browbeat their singers, adults as well as children, and they are sad, unco-operative singers as a result. Your choristers have come to your rehearsal to enjoy singing with you, and to take pride in what they will have achieved under your inspiring leadership.

So make your singers think. Try asking, for example, 'I can't hear any of the words in that passage – is it the vowels or the consonants that want improving?' That way you'll get both consonants and vowels improved!

But sometimes you have to demonstrate for them what they should do – such as, how to pronounce foreign words correctly, and why they need to sing this passage in a certain manner. Therefore your approach to your choral society and adult choir could be 50 per cent questions and 50 per cent instruction.

And, of course, the questions will tend to be rhetorical – 'Was that a good attack?', 'Are we all opening our mouths here?' You can't expect individual singers to shout out answers when you have a large choir in front of you.

On the other hand, when you continually tell your choir what to do they will automatically tend to go into Passive Mode. Passive Mode is the response preachers may get to some sermons – you just turn off while they go on talking for minutes on end.

Alas, I've found a number of enlightened choir directors – some of whom have read my books – who tell me that they know the importance of keeping their singers' interest alive by asking questions, but who spend the whole of their rehearsals telling their choirs what to do. As an observer I can see that their singers' attention is turned off. I even know of one choir where two of the adults in the back row regularly solve a crossword puzzle during their rehearsal. The conductor doesn't see them because she's too bound up by what she is saying – she's looking at her music most of the time, and only sees her singers as a sort of blur, rather than as individual people with whom she should be interacting.

Did you know that the singers in the front rows of your choir often sing better than those who sit further away from you? Are you aware of what is going on in the back rows of your choir, be it a church or school choir? There are two ways to ensure that the singers in the back rows pay as much attention to you as those who are sitting nearer to you.

1. Maintain creative and interactive eye contact with all your singers throughout your practice, especially with those who are sitting furthest from you. This means that, when your eyes meet, each of you knows what the other is thinking. If this does not happen during your rehearsals, you may need to work harder at your communication skills, i.e. being more friendly with singers when they are off duty, as well as ensuring that when you give a direction to your choir, everyone does it.

2. Configure the seating of your practice room so that you are able to walk along each row at least once during every rehearsal and can look every singer straight in the face while they are singing. This physical proximity will challenge all your singers to sing even better for you, especially if you can murmur a constructive comment or word of praise to individual singers – 'Push your lips a little further forward.' 'What a lovely sound.' 'Great breath control!' This will take courage on your part, but it will repay enormous dividends.

Never take 'Yes' for an answer

One more point about asking questions – if you do expect an answer from your singers, young or old, never accept 'Yes' as an adequate response. You see, if you ask a question such as, 'Did you understand that?', the answer will almost always be an automatic 'Yes'. The 'YES' means that the singer doesn't really want to be challenged to think about what you've just been asking them, and hopes that if they say 'Yes' you'll go on to something else.

So instead, ask questions which can't be answered by a simple 'Yes' or 'No', such as, 'What is it that you will get right?' That will provoke a thought-through answer which will help the singers actually to achieve what you want them to achieve.

It's sometimes a good idea, after you've made a point which will enable your choir to sing a passage better, to ask them, 'Why are we singing this again?' You may be surprised at the number of singers who don't know – who, therefore, hadn't been listening to what you were asking them to do. Try it.

Other choir skills

1. Processing

Does your choir process in an orderly manner? You will almost certainly be playing the organ when your choir processes so you won't be able to see them, but it is still your responsibility. Therefore, either appoint a senior choir member to look after this for you, and/or rehearse the processing yourself every few months, so that your choir knows that this is important to you – then it will become important to them.

Pay special attention to turning corners. If your choir has to make a right turn, almost certainly they will begin to veer to the left. The reason for this is that the singers immediately behind the choristers who are turning a corner, automatically try to get out of their way. This gradually builds up so that the choir veers more and more to one side. I've found that it is not only the young singers who develop this fault, but also, surprisingly, experienced adults. It will take a lot of tact and patience on your part to get them out of this habit.

2. Standing and sitting

Does your choir stand and sit together? If you rehearse this a couple of times at every practice, the choir's self-respect will immediately be enhanced, and it will also help them to be considerably more disciplined in their singing.

When your singers stand, have them stand in such a way that they are ready, *immediately*, to begin singing. Many singers move around for several seconds once they're standing. This not only wastes time, but it means that they're not really ready to sing. Let them rehearse 'standing to attention' and being really focused on what they are about to do. This will help them to achieve an even greater sense of corporate identity, and it will sharpen their own pride in what they are doing.

In church choirs which sing from choir stalls which face each other, appoint two leaders – one on each side. They can be a great help with the discipline of standing and sitting. When the hymn is announced, the leaders look at the singers on the opposite side of the choir to make sure they are ready – i.e. 'sitting to attention' – and then the leaders look at each other, one giving a slight nod, and with an imperceptible movement the leaders indicate that they are about to stand. One of the leaders should be the primary leader, and the other leader should take his or her time from the first.

When you rehearse your choir in the act of standing and sitting, let your leaders do it several times without you giving the order. Let the leaders take this responsibility during the rehearsal. And then, after you've rehearsed the whole anthem and rehearsed the choir in standing and sitting together, you might say, 'We're now going to sing the anthem right through, as for Sunday – I'll go to the organ, but you watch your leaders so that you'll know when to stand. And when we've finished singing, look at the leaders again to sit down together; and then we'll discuss how well it went.'

When I first tried this standing up and sitting down together with my village church choir they were very enthusiastic, but broke down in helpless laughter when they rehearsed it, because it was so new and such a fun thing to do. But the message got across that 'this is something which we ought to do', and so it succeeded. Let them take the initiative and they will be keen to respond – whether they're adults or children. Give them the responsibility and you'll not only find that they'll stand up and sit down better, but they'll sing better too.

Once your choir has accepted that they can stand and sit without you telling them to – and that they can do it much better that way – you can take this a step further by asking your leaders to nod their heads at each other for the beginnings and endings of verses of a hymn – after due rehearsal. ('We'll have two beats on the last note of each verse, then exactly two beats' rest before starting the next verse absolutely together. Let's practise that unaccompanied.') Once they have begun to achieve this, it will be your job, during services, to look at the beaters and take your time from them. In other words, your choir will have begun to take real responsibility for leading the music.

Your leaders will need some instruction on how to 'nod' effectively. Tell them that they should look at each other before the singing begins and when it is about to end, as well as at least once during every line of a hymn or four bars of music. You can't expect your singers to look at the leaders, if the leaders don't look at each other. They will find this difficult to do at first; but persevere, with kindness and tact, so that they may improve week by week.

When the choir has to sing a final chord for, say, four beats, your leaders should nod their heads, almost imperceptibly, for those final beats, as though nodding 'Yes': 'Nod, nod, nod, nod' ('Yes, yes, yes, yes'), so that the other singers can see and feel those four beats.

But, of course, a four-beat note comes off at the beginning of the fifth beat. In order to achieve this, your leaders should show, very clearly, when the final beat starts, so that the choir may finish together one beat later: 'Yes, yes, yes, *and* Off!

It's the 'and' beat which is the important one. Your leaders should push their heads slightly back for this penultimate 'nod', as though they were about to sneeze: '*Ah-choo*!' Once your beaters can do this easily and confidently, that four-beat chord will be sung very neatly indeed – 'Yes, yes, yes, *ah-choo*!

After this practice has established itself, and if your choir sings more than just congregational music, your beaters can take responsibility for conducting the sung responses and the Psalms. And the fruit of this will be that your choir will sing this 'bread and butter' music far better without you! You will have trained a choir which can take responsibility for its own singing.

3. Holding music

Have them hold their music well. Show them how to do this. Good stance is essential for good singing. Ask them, 'Show me how you should hold your books.' You may have to demonstrate to them how this may be done – with one hand acting as the book rest, and the other hand ready to turn the pages. The music should be held a little way from their bodies so that they can sing out horizontally (and not at the floor), and be able to see the music and each other at the same time. Also, books need to be held so that two pages are always open. Some choristers fold their music back upon itself, so that they can see only one page. This makes for untidy page-turning on their part and, of course, it doesn't do the music copy any good to be bent so far back.

4. Tidiness

Do the choir put their robes away neatly? Is the vestry tidy after services, or do you, as choir director, have to tidy up when your choir have left? Once you begin to do this for them, they will let you. Children especially need to be kept aware of the importance of tidiness and the care of robes. Have you appointed a robes person?

Are the choir stalls tidy after services? Perhaps someone could be appointed to look after this too. A pair of teenagers would welcome the responsibility, especially if you give them a title such as 'Choir-stall monitor', and show a regular interest in how they are helping you to motivate the choir.

Pep talks

Sometimes, when you want your choir to try especially hard, such as when they are about to sing a concert, you need to say something to enthuse and inspire them for their task – a pep talk.

I suggest that, when they are all lined up and about to process into their places, you say a few sentences which will encourage them to 'stand tall' and do even better than they think they can. You might say something like this:

'We've been practising for this concert for the last two months and you've all worked so hard. Thank you. In a few minutes' time we'll be sharing this fine music with our audience – there are a lot of people there waiting to hear us. I'm proud of you, and you'll be proud of yourselves. So hold your heads up high, smile, and enjoy every minute of it. Let's go!'

Joshua did the same when he was about to lead the children of Israel into the Promised Land: 'Be strong and of good courage!' Montgomery also did it before the battle of Alamein. And just as they were victorious, so will you and your choir be.

Professional musicians

Rehearsing a professional choir requires a different technique from rehearsing amateurs. Being trained singers, the professionals should be able to meet any requests you ask of them immediately. For example, you shouldn't have to ask them more than once to sing softly or not to breathe in a certain place. They will have the same professional status as you – therefore talk to them as adult to adult, courteously and concisely.

By the way, when a soloist has to sing or play an aria or solo, it is they who set the *tempo*, not the conductor. Give way to their wishes regarding that part of your performance.

Should you have to discuss a point with a solo professional singer during a dress rehearsal with your choral society and orchestra, always make your suggestions to him or her one on one, and not publicly. You would not wish to be corrected in front of your singers, so give a similar courtesy to your professional soloist.

Humour

Archbishop Robert Runcie once said that nobody should be put in charge of anything unless he has a sense of humour. If you have a natural sense of humour, the introduction of a laugh during your concentrated rehearsal can work like a refreshing shower on a hot day. These touches of humour needn't necessarily be helpfully constructive – as you can see from some of my unguarded remarks, written down by one of my choirmen in America.

When rehearsing Byrd's four-part *Mass*: 'Choir, please sing this as though Byrd were quite a good composer.'

When singing plainsong: 'Gentlemen, you sound like monks who have lost their vocation.'

'Trebles, will you try to look, for want of a better word, competent?'

'Altos, you sound damp.'

'Tenors, please don't sound as though you've been used as bait.'

'Basses, don't sound as though you're auditioning to be second foghorn on the *Queen Mary*.'

Let your practices, therefore, be filled with smiles. They'll make the hard work even more rewarding.

CHAPTER 22

Random hints for church choir practice

1. Rehearsing hymns

If your choir gets bored with rehearsing hymns and finds them dull, the reason may be that you yourself find them dull. What interests you will interest your choir. If you consciously approach your choir rehearsals feeling not only excited about the music you will rehearse and full of good humour, but knowing that you and your choir will actually enjoy the process, you're halfway to achieving a really worthwhile rehearsal.

I once attended a church choir rehearsal where the director got his choir to sing all the verses of all the hymns all the way through without any constructive comments. It was incredibly boring – he had no idea what to rehearse or how to rehearse it. With his permission I stepped in and showed him and his choir how to rehearse in fine detail. We rehearsed only one verse of one hymn and a verse from another hymn. By introducing one challenge at a time, I encouraged them, with a smile:

(a) To sing together. 'Sing the first note to the vowel "Ee" and come in together, unaccompanied, with my beat: One, two, ready, breathe!' Of course, I had to ask them to try this a second or even a third time until I, and they, knew that they had achieved what I had asked of them. This kind of repetition and reinforcement is needed in all details of choir training.

(b) To blend and balance. 'Sing that first chord again and listen to each other. Can you hear the other voices around you? Perhaps some of you need to sing a little more softly, and some a little more courageously.'

(c) To sing the right notes. 'Now sing the tune all through unaccompanied to "Ah" with the back of your throat open . . . Altos, there was a problem in the second line. What was it? Let's get it right – once with the piano, then on your own, and then all together.'

(d) To start each new phrase together. 'Still singing to "Ah", breathe only at the end of every four bars, and cut the note at the end of each phrase slightly short, so that you have plenty of time to breathe and you can come in firmly together on the first note of the next phrase . . . Some of you are still hanging on to each last note of the phrases; it's the *next* note that's the important one.'

(e) To breathe so that they make sense of the words.
'Now sing the first verse, breathing only where you ought
to – look at the punctuation . . . Some of you are still
breathing in the middle of the second line: *Once for
favoured* (breath) *sinners slain*.'

(f) To sing with crystal-clear diction. 'I can't hear the "d"
on the word "thousanD".'

(g) To sing the meaning of the words. 'There's a long
note in the middle of the first line: *When I sur-vey the
won-drous cross* . . . What will you do with it?' [Answer:
'*Crescendo* through "vey" to the first syllable of "*won-
drous*".']

(h) To hold their books proudly. 'You sound great, but do
you look great? How are you holding your books?'

(i) To become responsible, thinking singers. 'Can you
apply what you've achieved in that hymn to the next one?
. . . What didn't you do there?'

(j) To look pleasant. 'Look at the singers on the other side
of the choir and tell me if their faces would encourage the
congregation to come to church regularly!'

Their singing improved immediately and they found that
a choir practice – even when practising hymns – could be
an exciting and worthwhile experience.

In hymns the climax of a verse is often found in the last
line ('. . . who died to save us all'; '. . . praise with us the
God of grace'; '. . . Jesus Christ, her little child'). But, so
often, choirs tend to run out of breath at these moments,
and so they sing less firmly. Choir directors need to point
this out – frequently – to their singers to ensure that the
message of that crucial part of a verse is sung with convic-
tion, not with apathy.

The secret of all good choir training is to concentrate on
details. Let the singers feel that their singing is becoming
more and more focused, like a good clear photograph. As
with a well-focused photograph you can see the minute
details, so with a well-focused choir you can hear the fine
detail.

These things don't just apply to hymns, of course, but to
everything your choir sings. I have explained all of them
in detail elsewhere in this book, especially in Chapter 14,
but in general terms your aims when rehearsing your
church choir could be summed up as follows:

   i. Encourage your choir to sing confidently.
  ii. Help your choir to sing accurately.
 iii. Inspire your choir to sing intelligently.

Sometimes I'm asked whether church choirs should sing the hymns in unison or in harmony. That depends on the ability of your choir. If they can sing in harmony pretty accurately, by all means have them sing in four parts. If they have a problem with that, have them sing the tune only. It's good practice, by the way, to have the first and last verses of hymns sung in unison for services. That will help give the congregation a good lead – which is one reason why there's a choir.

2. Write notes on Sunday to help your choir on Friday

By working on fine details week by week, your choir will gradually improve the quality of their singing and will take increasing pride in their achievements. They will also look forward to their next rehearsal so that they can learn even more from you.

I find it very helpful to have a notebook and pencil with me at the organ on Sundays so that I can write down the things that went well and also the things that need more polish. I bring those notes with me to our next practice so that my singers will know that I really care.

I compliment them on what they have done well and show how pleased I am that they are making such good progress. Then I ask them what they think didn't go right. Having to think about it for themselves helps them to take more responsibility for their own singing. And then we set about putting those wrong things right, ready for next Sunday. In this way, improvement goes on all the time.

Of course, if something goes very badly wrong it's important that you, as the choir director, take full blame for it and don't unload the blame onto your singers. You are the captain of the ship and everything that happens, be it good or bad, is your responsibility. Let them take the credit for singing well; when things go wrong, let them know that they went wrong because you didn't make it wholly easy for them. This will make them want to please you even more.

3. Don't play the organ for choir practice

An organ is not a helpful instrument to play for a rehearsal; it can drown what the singers are doing and, almost certainly, you'll have your back to your choir when you're playing. So use a piano. Or, better still, borrow an electronic keyboard. Then you will be able to stand in the middle of your singers, continually making eye contact with them, and really hearing what they are doing. You can't lead a rehearsal when you have your back to your singers, or when they have their backs to you.

4. Sing incorrectly on purpose

It can sometimes be very helpful to get your choir to sing incorrectly on purpose. If, for example, they tend to breathe in the wrong place: 'When other helpers (breath) fail and comforts flee.' Ask them to sing it that way deliberately. They'll all laugh when they've done it. Then get them to sing it correctly, and you'll find that it will be right on Sunday. This works for adults as well as children.

Similarly, it's sometimes helpful, if your choristers are not really singing the message of the words sufficiently creatively, to get them to sing a different word. 'There is a *blue* hill far away, *within* a city wall . . . ' When they sing it with the correct words ('There is a *green* hill far away, *without* a city wall . . . ') they'll find that the word 'green' has a new element of greenness about it, and the word 'without' will mean 'outside' rather than 'not having'.

Doing this occasionally can lift the spirits of your choir and give them not only a new insight into the importance of understanding the meaning of the text, but also add a much needed moment of humour to your rehearsals. ('Come let us join our *boring* songs . . . '; '*Half* my hope on God is founded . . . '; 'In the *warm* mid-*summer* frosty wind made moan . . . ')

5. Singing in colour

While on the subject of singing words with meaning, choirs need to realise that many adjectives and nouns have within themselves the spirit of their meaning, which is waiting to be 'realised' (made real) by the singers. For example, 'red' will have the spirit of redness if the 'R' is rolled or trilled: 'Rrrrred'. 'Green' will sound cool when the vowels 'ee' are slightly prolonged: 'Greeeen'. 'Still' will have the spirit of peace if the 'S' is prolonged and the 'T' emphasised: 'Ssss-Till'.

On the other hand, it's possible to impute the wrong feeling to a word. 'White' can sound 'black' if spoken deeply, and 'black' can sound 'white' if spoken with a high voice, gently. It's up to the choir director to ensure that all words are sung with appropriate colour: black must sound black and white must sound white.

When your choir sings 'God' (*Blessed be the God and Father* . . .) that word must have a spirit of awe and majesty and wonder, rather than sound ineffectually neutral when it is sung softly at the beginning of this classic anthem.

The secret of singing words in colour is two-fold: a) Whenever possible, lean on the initial consonants, such as 'Llllove', 'Blllue', 'Ooooowonder', 'Prrrraise'; and

b) Sing *through* these words making a small, but steadily forward-moving *crescendo* towards the next important syllable. ('Blllessed be the Go——d and *Fa*ther of our Lllor—d *Je*sus Christ . . . ')

6. Smile, please

Encourage you singers to smile – or, at the very least, look pleasant when they're singing. Singers who have half a smile and who raise their eyebrows when singing (instead of frowning) immediately make a better sound.

Try it. Have your singers frown when singing a line of a hymn. Then get them to raise their eyebrows, looking slightly surprised, with a half smile. Then ask them which sounded better.

CHAPTER 23

Rehearsal techniques at a glance

1. **Do your homework**, so that you will know what you are going to rehearse and how you will rehearse it.

2. **Be excited** at the prospect of the good things that will happen during your practice.

3. **Arrive early**, to prepare the room and chat with your singers.

4. **Start punctually** with a cheerful greeting.

5. **Begin with easy warm-ups**, which the choir can sing well.

6. **Challenge your choir to sing even better** within the first few seconds.

7. **Insist that all singers begin everything they sing absolutely together** (warm-ups, hymns, anthems), by breathing exactly one beat before they sing.

8. **Get your choir to think for themselves** by asking them questions every fifteen or thirty seconds throughout the rehearsal.

9. **Cover the ten points** we have discussed in Chapter 14, pages 62-83.

10. **Practise sight-reading.** Insert at least a couple of one-minute periods of sight-reading instruction in every practice.

11. **Maintain eye-to-eye contact with your singers.** Conduct them with the expression on your face as well as with the wave of your hands. Teach them to respond to your signals.

12. **Mix standing and sitting** – but make sure your singers don't slouch.

13. **Mix good humour with a high standard of self-discipline.** Your singers want to enjoy their practices and also to get satisfaction from their achievements.

14. **Give your singers a half-time break.** They need to be able to relax, if you're working them as hard as you should. But make the break constructive by giving out notices or asking if anyone has something to say.

15. **Finish punctually,** with a smiling 'Well done, and thank you!' and stay to talk with your singers afterwards.

CHAPTER 24

Searching questions which demand action

Is the piano in my practice room tuned regularly? If not, how can I expect my choir to sing in tune?

Can the accompanist see me when I'm conducting?

Is the accompanist playing the piano too loudly, thus leading the singing rather than supporting it?

Do I play the piano too loudly and too much, thus taking the responsibility for leading the singing from the choir?

Do I realise that when I am conducting the choir, they are following the accompanist and not me?

Am I sure that I am looking at my choir when I conduct them, or do I drop my eyes to the safety of the music when I bring them in?

When did I last conduct some music from memory – or do I always keep the music in front of me, 'just in case'?

Do I lead my practices by staying safely behind the piano, or do I venture out to stand close to the singers so that I can really hear what they are doing and so help them to sing even better?

Have I really given my very best to tonight's practice? Do I love the music I've given them to sing? Do I love every one of my singers? Or am I afraid of some of them?

Did my choir sing better this week than they did last week? Did they learn a new technique from me this week?

What did I learn from tonight's rehearsal which will enable me to lead next week's practice more efficiently?

Do I lead practices so that my singers are enthused by the high standards I set and the attractive leadership I give, or do I browbeat them? They only come to choir because they want to; am I helping them to want to?

How is the balance in my rehearsals between my talking and the choir singing, especially at the beginning of practices? Do I quickly get my choir singing so that they can feel that they are actually doing something positive – within the first few seconds of the rehearsal?

Do I know the names of all my singers and those of their families? When did I last visit them, or ask them round to my house?

Do I really listen when people talk to me, or am I too bound up in myself? Do I realise they are paying me the compliment of sharing a concern with me – not necessarily for me to do anything about it, but just to give them a listening ear? How is my body language when I'm listening? Do I look at them, or look over their shoulder?

When did we last have a choir party or take the choir to sing somewhere else?

Is my practice room always tidy? Does its neatness make it welcoming to my singers?

Do I meet with my minister regularly, so that misunderstandings are less likely to arise?

Is there any part of my choir's life which is disorganised and a mess? Hadn't I better do something about it now?

Is my choir library kept neatly? Is the librarian efficient? If not, is it because I need to encourage him more frequently and to be more efficient myself?

How is the balance between my professional life and my family life, bearing in mind that no one at the end of their life ever wished they had spent more time in the office?

Is there a problem in my life that I haven't faced, in the hope that it will just go away?

Am I nannying my choir by thinking that they can't do anything unless I'm there to help them? Do I conduct them when they don't need conducting? Do I think I'm indispensable or am I making myself dispensable? Am I educating them, individually and corporately, so that I can take pride in stepping back to watch them take responsibility for their own singing?

How many times do I play a chord when the choir has to repeat a passage? Do they really need it?

Do I make every effort to look neat on Sundays? Is there a dress code for the choir, including footwear which can easily be seen under choir robes, or does anything go?

Does my choir look as though they believe the words they sing and say? Are they giving a strong lead to the congregation not only musically but also spiritually? Do they look joyful or worried when they are singing?

What am I doing to foster good relations between choir and congregation?

When did I last sit in the congregation for a service so that I could assess how the choir and organ really sound?

How many of the congregation do I know by name?

Do I attend non-musical events at my church on a regular basis?

Do I actively seek good relationships with the other musicians in the town?

Am I sometimes so busy that I haven't the time to say 'Good morning' to people I see at church or in the church office?

What am I doing about that person in my choir that I don't really like, and of whom, therefore, I am secretly afraid? Do I realise that it's up to me, not to him, to put this right?

How efficient is my paperwork?

Is my organ console really tidy? When did I last clean the keys and polish the pedals?

Am I looking after myself physically, emotionally and spiritually? Is there someone in my life with whom I can share my problems, and from whom I can receive wise counsel?

How many of these faults does my choir have?

> Arriving late
> Absent without excuse
> No real sense of expectation on arrival
> Not listening when I ask them to do something
> Talking when I am talking
> Not starting together
> Not standing and sitting together
> Not making a pleasant sound
> Breathing in the wrong places
> Singing wrong notes
> Singing out of tune
> Not looking at me when I'm conducting.

Well, you know who has to help them cure those faults, don't you?

Do I pray for my singers and minister regularly and thank God for the privilege of being entrusted with such a wonderful vocation?

CHAPTER 25

Running a children's choir

Starting a children's choir

If you want to start a children's choir, and you know there is a real need for one in your town, ask yourself the following questions so that you'll have a clearer idea of what it is that you want to create.

1. What age group do you want your choir to cater for?

You need to be selective. A choir made up of children of all ages poses too many difficulties, i.e. very young children would not be able to sing the same demanding music which older children could manage. And the older children would probably not have the patience to wait while you taught the younger ones the notes.

The only way to have a choir made up of a wide age range would be to rehearse them in separate peer groups, and that would take up a lot of time. No – initially you need to limit your choir to a particular age group.

But that raises questions as to what you will do when those children are one year, or two or more years older. Boys' voices will change – will you form a senior choir of ATBs with them, or just let them go? Girls' voices get better and better. Will you want to lose them, or to keep them until they leave school?

2. Do you want boys and girls in your choir?

Ask yourself how the boys will relate to the girls and vice versa – for girls become physically developed more quickly than boys, and so you need to know how you're going to handle that. Some boys regard singing in choirs as a not very masculine activity. You will have to show them that it's as challenging as playing football or tennis, so that they'll value what you plan to give them.

3. How will you go about recruiting your young singers?

First you have to find a nucleus – either from your church or from a nearby school. Once you have got your nucleus you can then use those children to recruit other children: the best recruiters for any children's choir are the children who are already in it. (The same applies to recruiting adults to your adult choir.)

If you make their membership really worthwhile, they will naturally want their friends to join too. I know of one superb church choir in the USA that has a fabulous programme which includes a foreign tour every two years. That same choir also has a policy which requires that every child shall bring one new child to join the choir every year, and it works very successfully. It's a policy well worth considering for your choir too.

I also know of a parish church choir near where I live in Lancashire, led by a dynamic choir director, which has a membership of twenty men and forty boys – and a waiting list. They not only sing worthwhile music for Sunday services, but they also sing in the Isle of Man for a week after Easter, and they go to France for a week in the summer. Success breeds success; and so you will need to think ambitiously when planning the activities of your children's choir.

When you've established your choir, make a video of them and send copies to all potential members for your new intake: 'You could sing like this; you could enjoy the experience of working with us; you could visit lovely places like this.' Also print coloured postcards of the choir and send one to each new member who has auditioned (see 4 below). 'We look forward to welcoming you . . .'.

But meanwhile, you will, of course, try the well-worn methods of advertising in your church magazine, and getting articles in the newspaper with photographs of a small group of your children looking angelic (that always attracts a lot of attention). By the way, never say, 'There are lots of vacancies.' That gives the impression you are desperate for members and are not very successful. Say instead, 'There are only a few vacancies.' That not only gives the impression of success, but it will also imply that if candidates don't apply right now, they'll be too late.

4. Auditions

When you meet potential new members of your choir for the first time, your challenge is so to enthuse them by what they can achieve with you in five or ten minutes that they will actively begin to be more eager to join your choir. Therefore I do suggest that you audition them in twos or threes, not to discover how gifted they are, but to reveal to them, and to you, that working creatively together is a wonderful and worthwhile experience. So, let your approach to them be friendly, dynamic and challenging:

(a) Welcome them

Ask them questions about themselves – their hobbies and other interests. Get them talking to you. (Let their parents watch from the other end of the room, so that you may the more easily build up a friendly, co-operative atmosphere.)

(b) Pitch

See if they can pitch single notes played on the piano, starting on G above middle C. If they can, then almost certainly you'll accept them – but don't tell them that yet. Let them gradually realise that working with you is fun. (Some children find that it is easier to pitch a note which is sung to them, rather than played on the piano.)

If children find it hard to match pitch, play the note that they sang, instead, and go on from there.

(c) Rhythm

Have them sustain a single note for four counts, coming off on five. (Count on your fingers while they do this, so that they know exactly what is required of them.)

(d) Questions

Once you have given them an instruction which they don't quite manage to fulfil, always follow it up with a question: 'Did you sing too high or too low?', 'Did you come off exactly on "five" or nearly on "five"? Try it again.' Never tell them that what they did was incorrect – let them tell you. They will be thrilled to discover that they are learning so much for themselves by working with you.

I aimed at making this brief audition period into a game of 'musical tennis'. I would lob a ball to the children (an easy question), so that they could lob it straight back at me (a right answer). I would then throw a different question to them, which needed a sung response.

This lively interaction quickly had them on their toes, mentally, for they realised that I was indeed a musical sports coach for them; and they enjoyed the game, for they learned so much from it.

(Rehearsals for the full children's choirs were also conducted on 'musical tennis' lines, and these became times when the children's skills increased markedly week by week as I lobbed them increasingly demanding shots, mixed, of course, with easier ones.)

(e) More

And so gently expand the demands you are making on the children you are auditioning. Increase the counting to five beats: ('Coming off on . . .?'). Then gradually, say, up to ten, raising each note by a semitone each time. Children love to respond to a challenge.

(f) Mouth

Have them sing these single notes to a clear 'Ah': ('Was your mouth wholly open, or rather shut?') Show them how to drop their jaw easily, by putting two, and then three fingers in their mouth.

(g) Song

If there's time have them sing a verse of a simple song or hymn which they know – and show them how they can sing at least one part of it better: ('How many beats on that last note? Let's try it again.'; 'Can you sing that line in one breath?'; 'What letter did you miss out on the word "an*d*"? Let's have another go.')

By this time they should feel excited by all that they have achieved with you. They will have sung better with you in five minutes than they've ever done before. This will really strengthen their wish to join your choir to see what they can achieve next time. So have a word with their parents and ask if they'd like their children to come to the next practice to see what it's like to work with the other children. (This will give them the freedom still to say 'No' – don't push them into a corner by saying that they must join the choir. It will be up to them to tell you that this is what they want.)

But it will be up to you to make their first full rehearsal so rewarding that they will want to come to the next one, and the next, and the one after that. And you do that by asking lots of questions which all the children can answer, and also by working with the new members in small groups, in a carefully thought-through programme of education.

By the way, when you first see a child, never ask him or her if they want to join your choir, for the answer will nearly always be 'No'. They haven't experienced what it's like, so give them a taste of that experience by the way in which you lead their audition.

5. How many rehearsals will you have?

Will you have one practice a week or two, and how long will they be? Two practices a week is a good idea for children's choirs, because it helps to keep the impetus going. One practical way to achieve this is to dedicate the second rehearsal to the teaching of sight-reading and vocal production to small groups. The ability to read music is one of the surest ways of enthusing singers and of retaining them through the teenage years. Working in small groups of three or four is also a sure way to build up creative relationships with your singers.

I know of one conductor of a major church in California who had only one rehearsal with his children – on Sunday mornings before the service. After I had led a week's choral workshop for his boys and girls I suggested that he should double the number of rehearsals if he wanted to enable his choristers to sing even better. He doubted if this was a practical possibility, for it had never been done before and many singers had to travel long distances to the church. However, he did offer four extra practices each week at which children, in small groups, would be taught sight-reading and vocal techniques. The children could come to any two. He telephoned me a few weeks later to say that not only did all the children find that these special rehearsals were excitingly and creatively worthwhile, but that some of the children were so keen that they came to all four rehearsals!

You may think that your children couldn't afford the time because they have so many other commitments, but you will find that if you run a really well-organised programme which makes high demands on the children, and from which they reap high rewards, they will be keen to make the time.

I ran such choirs in the USA for sixteen years, in a university town where tremendous demands were made upon children academically and socially, and also competitively in sports – and yet some of them came to three practices a week plus Sundays. (You can read about those choirs in my other books.)

A 45-minute rehearsal is long enough for most young children. When they are a little older, and have more experience, an hour or even longer is possible. It's amazing how long children can work if they are continually challenged to raise their standards, and encouraged, through your creative questions, to 'own' the progress they are making.

6. How are you going to finance your choir?

Don't think that it won't cost much to run a children's choir. What about the cost of music? What about the hire of a practice room? What about the cost of photocopying and mailing letters to the children's families to keep them up to date with your schedule? What about paying for an accompanist? And, once your choir has become established, what about the cost of hiring a coach to take them to sing at concerts? If your choir are to wear robes, that will need considerable finance.

The matter of finance implies that you must have a treasurer; and having a treasurer implies that you must have a committee to which he or she will be answerable; and having a committee means that you will need to decide how you will set it up and who will be the chairperson.

One of the most important people on your committee will be your publicity officer – someone who knows how to promote your choir in the newspapers and on local radio, so that you will attract not only new singers but also large audiences which, in their turn, will generate financial support. There's nothing so exciting as to sing to a large responsive audience. And there's nothing so depressing as singing to a nearly empty hall, and nothing so frustrating as to have continual cash-flow problems. Your publicity person will indeed be a key member of your team. So there's a lot to think about.

When I was leading choral workshops in Australia I conducted several rehearsals with the Australian Youth Choirs, which at that time had three thousand members. They were superbly organised by a full-time staff and they gave concerts not only all over Australia, but abroad as well. They'd sung in Westminster Abbey, they'd sung in the USA, and they'd sung for the Pope.

They managed to do all that because they charged each parent a reasonable termly fee for the privilege of their child singing in those choirs. That fee paid for the appointment of conductors, the hiring of practice rooms, the buying of music and the organisation of concerts and overseas tours.

That fee also meant that parents would ensure that their children attended rehearsals regularly, so as to get their money's worth. It's a general rule in life that people only appreciate what they pay for. If it's free, then it's valued less. In fact, instead of paying children to sing in the choir, as some churches do, we could think about doing the reverse, and charge them. At the very least, when starting a choir, an entrance fee could encourage commitment.

If you are giving them something of value which will last them all their lives, then it will be worth the while of parents to pay. They'll appreciate so much more what you are giving to their children and, of course, they'll also be more motivated to keep you up to the mark.

A graded training scheme

I do suggest that you establish a clear scheme whereby your children can work their way through a graded system of training – rather like scouts or guides – getting little rewards for a test passed or an objective achieved. One of my choir-director friends in Rhode Island told me that her 4-year-old singers could read music better than they could read words. It's so simple to teach children to read music and in the long run it makes the directing of rehearsals so much easier, for the children can sing right notes almost immediately.

When you teach your new children musical theory, please teach them round a piano, so that the theory can become immediately practical. When you are teaching key signatures, for example, actually show your children an F sharp when talking about the key of G major. Let them play the scale of G for themselves, with, and also without, the F sharp, so that they can both hear and see how and why that scale needs an F sharp. I've found, alas, that even in some enlightened cathedrals the teaching of theory is done round a table, and there's nothing so dull as unrelieved theory.

Teach the children by asking them the right questions as often as you can. It's so exciting to see children, as well as adults, transform themselves through being made to think for themselves and discover that they already knew what they should do, but hadn't realised it until they were asked the right questions.

If the choir director is wholly committed to a scheme of training, it will really work; and it will also mean that you will be more likely to keep your children in the choir until they leave school at the age of 18, because an ongoing training scheme will have made it worth their while to stay with you through those important years.*

If your children are not used to giving their whole-hearted attention to what you ask of them, you may find that it will be difficult to get them out of their lackadaisical attitude. I recently led some rehearsals for a nationally respected children's choir. They could sing quite well, but it was like drawing teeth to get them to give me their full attention. Their own conductor had accepted a low standard of concentration for so long. It took me twice as long as I expected to achieve what I asked of them.

So, if you are enthused to expect the very best from all of your children, keep striving for this, however hard it may seem.

As I've said before, directing a choir is like training a sports team; you have to build up the team gradually over a period of time. So when you start a new choir, aim for a

* The Royal School of Church Music has a practical scheme of graded training for singers of all ages, called *Voice for Life*. E-mail: voiceforlife@rscm.com Website: www.rscm.com

clearly defined goal which the singers can reach in the first few months, such as singing a few songs at a small concert, fully supported by choir parents. (You'll need a committee member to be in charge of choir-parent liaison.) This will give your singers a terrific boost in morale, which will enable you to aim for a more ambitious concert next time.

Always have in mind that you are the coach of this team – and they will respond to every challenge that you give them if you know how to enable them to meet those challenges. The more you ask of them, the more they will give. People always respond to a challenge. If you expect only low standards then it's not really worth the while of your singers to turn out on a wet Monday night to attend your rehearsals, is it?

Teaching children to read music

One thing I would beg of you: always give your children copies with music. So many children are given only the words when they learn songs, which means, alas, that they are being taught by rote, and are not being trained to be musically literate. They may be able to sing their music well under such a scheme, but they won't know how to do it after they've left your choir – and that's what you ought to aim for. Make it your long-term goal to educate singers to be musically literate, so that when they grow up they will be able to pass on to the next generation the skills they learned from you.

Therefore, I cannot stress too much or often the importance of teaching young singers to read music – for three reasons:

1. It makes the leading of choir practices so much easier for the conductor.

2. It makes choir practices so much more interesting for the young singers.

3. It gives the singers a valuable gift which will remain with them for the rest of their lives.

Once you have begun to teach your young people to read music, all you have to do when you hand them a piece of music is to say, 'Sing it!' and they will be able to.

Just before I left my Episcopal Church in Princeton I received a letter from a choral director in New Zealand asking if he could watch our rehearsals for a week. I was staggered that he wanted to fly halfway round the world to see our music programme. At our first rehearsal he watched an 8-year-old girl sing absolutely correctly, unaccompanied, four bars of music which she hadn't seen before. He said, 'That's made my trip worthwhile.'

At our last practice, several days later, he watched my choir of sixty volunteer men, boys and senior girls sight-read Stanford's *Magnificat* and *Nunc Dimittis* in A (which we'd never sung before) absolutely correctly and with all the expression. I was tremendously proud of them – my guest was thrilled, and so were all my singers.

Another choir director told me that, until she'd watched my Princeton boys and girls read music so easily, she hadn't realised that when singers can read music, the choir director can begin straight away to polish the singing rather than have to spend time teaching the notes.

Teaching sight-singing

There are a few simple steps to take at every practice which will eventually enable your singers, both adults and children, to read music. (A chalk board or flipchart is a very useful tool for teaching.)

1a. Teach them how to clap simple rhythms which can be found in any hymn book – crotchets, minims and semibreves (quarter notes, half and whole notes).

1b. Put what they have learned into immediate practice by getting them to clap the rhythm of a few bars of a new anthem. When they have done that successfully, get them to do it again while you play the tune with them. Thus they will realise the connection between what they have clapped and the music they are about to sing.

2a. Teach them the basics of pitch: five lines, clef, and music moving in step – alternate lines and spaces. Also repeated notes.

2b. Put this into immediate practice by challenging them to work out, without help from the keyboard, the pitch of a few bars of simple, unfamiliar music. Don't bother about rhythm at this stage. They will find it helpful to point to the notes they are singing, so that they can feel their 'upness' and 'downness'.

3a. Once they have begun to master these basics, hardly ever play the tune when accompanying them on the piano. Play only the harmony. This will spur them to try even harder.

3b. If you do habitually play the melody line when learning new music, your singers will imitate you so quickly that both you and they will think that they are reading the music. They are not!

4a. Whenever you present a piece of music to be sung, ask your choristers to look at the first note, telling you its alphabetical name and how many beats it is worth. Then, without you playing that note, ask them to attempt to pitch it for themselves.

It does not matter so much if the note they pitch is a hit or a miss. What matters is that you will be training them to look at the notes creatively. And that's what sight-singing is all about.

4b. Then play that first chord and challenge them to sing the first few bars unaccompanied. Thus you will be training them continually to think for themselves.

5. Throughout the practice, whenever a wrong note is sung, ask first what the error is, and second who will attempt to sing it correctly (without any help from the piano). Thus your singers will be encouraged to grow musically at every rehearsal.

6. Gradually introduce additional teaching when it is needed: more complex rhythms and pitch (skill in sol-fa can be very helpful), accidentals, rests, expression marks, etc.

7. Beware of doing the thinking for your choir: 'You sang an F instead of an F sharp. This is what an F sharp sounds like.' Once you get into the habit of doing this, your singers will abruptly cease to think for themselves and their skill in reading music will begin to deteriorate.

Once you've begun to teach your singers the art of sight-singing, it's important that you allow them to put into practice what they have learned. A few years ago I led a week's workshop for choral directors in the USA – there were over a hundred there. One of them told me that she spent ten minutes of every rehearsal teaching her children to read music. I was delighted to hear this. But then she added, 'Of course, when we rehearse the music, I have to teach the notes by rote, for there isn't time to waste while they try to work them out for themselves.'

No wonder her children can't sight-read music. It's the same with any activity. You have to put into practice what you have learned, otherwise it's all theory. You can read as many books as you like on dieting and know all about calories, but unless you actually begin to diet in practice, you won't lose weight. You can read books about exercise, but unless you actually do it, your health will not improve.

It's exactly the same with learning to read music. By all means teach your children, step by step, how to do it in theory. But unless they are actually allowed to try it for themselves during regular rehearsals – which involve them making mistakes and correcting them on their own – they will never succeed, for they'll know that you will take the responsibility of thinking for them.

It's so simple to teach young singers to read music if you have a passion for it;* and once they've learned how, it makes rehearsals so much more enjoyable – both for you and for them.

Teaching children to sing high notes

Singing high notes is not really difficult for children – they often do it in the playground, when they call 'Coo-ee' to other children. So when they're round the piano with you get them to sing a 'whoop' from a note around G above middle C and scoop up as high as they can and then scoop down again, to a 'Wow'. (Some choir directors call this a 'siren'.) Get them to do it three or four or five times so that they can progressively get rid of their inhibitions.

Some children will only manage to go up four or five notes to around a D or E. That's OK. But others will soar much higher – even to a top C or above – and they'll do it so easily.

Your task will be to ask them, individually, to sing another siren and to realise how easy it is. Then you will play them the highest note that they have sung (this will require some pretty quick thinking on your part) and ask them to sing, with very light accompaniment, a downwards scale from that top note to 'Ah'. They must do it immediately, before they've had time to think to themselves, 'This is a high note; I can't sing high notes!'

Not all the children will be able to manage this at first, but a few will, especially the younger ones. And so you need to build on this foundation each week, perhaps finishing your warm-ups with a few 'sirens'. These will not only help your children to relax, but also they will encourage them to know that high notes are there for each and every one of them to enjoy.

When I first tried this with a group of 8-year-old girls in Princeton, one of the smallest girls was able to sing me a three-octave scale from a top-top A flat to the A flat below

---

* See my *Five Wheels to Successful Sight-singing*, published by Augsburg Fortress, USA. There is also a video available. (Obtainable from the RSCM: musicsupplies@rscm.com or from Clifford Hill: chmusic@idt.net)

middle C. I was amazed, but she thought it was quite natural – which, of course, it was.

Research findings

A study about the teaching of music to very young children was recently released from the University of California. It came to the inescapable conclusion that when music training is begun early, especially learning the piano, it actually boosts a child's brainpower.

The researchers found that musical training, as early as the age of 3, enhanced children's overall mental ability. They said that babies are born with certain brain cells that respond to musical sounds, and that these neurons grow in patterns which can be expanded to perform increasingly complex interactions – a kind of pre-language which the brain can develop even before verbal language skills.

They reached these conclusions by testing pre-school children from 3 to 5 years old, and they found that after only six months of lessons on little pianos, the children showed dramatic improvement in solving spacial reasoning tests which are central in the study of mathematics and science. They came to the conclusion that music had stimulated the formation of new and permanent connections in the children's brains.

The researchers also made a study which compared the response of children who worked with computers with the response of children who were having piano lessons. They were amazed to discover that the piano students tested 35 per cent better than the children who concentrated on their computer studies alone.

The head teacher of one of the schools where this research was carried out said that after only six months the children who received the piano instruction were able to focus to a greater degree, and were able to be more centred and to do better in their general studies than the other children.

The connection between music and mathematics has long been recognised, and this research suggests that when children are trained in musical skills from a very early age their mathematical prowess also increases.

Child protection

When adults work with children, in schools, clubs or choirs, the legal requirements of the Children Act must be observed. This protects both the children and their teachers, and it also gives reassurance to the parents.

For example, an adult is not allowed to give first aid to a child unless permission has been given by the child's parents beforehand. Choir directors need, therefore, to be made aware of the requirements of this Act.

Basically it requires that every teacher fills in a legal form concerning his or her history of working with children; furthermore, there should at least be one adult present, in addition to the leader, at every rehearsal. A rota of choir parents might be arranged to cover this. Make sure that supervising parents arrive early and don't leave until the last child has left the room.

A choir director should never be alone with a child – even accidentally – for this could lay him or her wide open to unpleasant accusations.

For further information consult your local education authority. The Royal School of Church Music (RSCM) and the Incorporated Society of Musicians (ISM) also have helpful guidelines readily available. Their addresses may be found in the Appendix.

CHAPTER 26

Problems with clergy – and others

What do you do if your minister doesn't agree with your choice of music, or with the way you run the choir? What if he or she tells you to play music you don't like? What if some of the adults in your choir are difficult to get on with, or you have problems with the parents of some of your young singers?

Well, here are some of the things you should *not* do in situations of personal conflict, and some of the things you should – plus some of the dangers you need to be aware of.

1. Never complain to all and sundry

Ninety-nine people out of a hundred generally complain about their problems to people who can't do anything about them – just to have a good moan. This solves nothing, and can often make matters worse, not only because you're not tackling the problem directly, but also because your complaining reinforces your own frustration and negative feelings; thus the problem becomes bigger in your mind and still remains unresolved.

If you need to talk to someone else about your difficulties, go to a trusted friend, or a person in authority, who might be able to help you. You will then begin to see a way forward.

But most important of all, talk to the person who is at the heart of your problem. Only then can you hope to work out some kind of effective solution. But beware – never approach that person with an angry determination to get your own way. Confrontation is the worst possible approach. But if you step out boldly, determined to work *with* others rather than against them, almost certainly you'll be able to solve most, if not all, of the problems that come your way.

2. Never argue

Never argue in writing

The written word is so much stronger than the spoken word. So every letter that you exchange about your disagreements will serve only to entrench you and your 'opponent' in the conflicting positions you hold. Once you put on paper, 'You said so and so and you're wrong', you immediately set up the situation for a battle, because the other person will write back to you to justify him or herself. And that will lead you to answer in stronger terms, and so the situation will quickly get out of hand for both of you. You will be like children who say, 'Yes, you did', 'No I didn't'; 'Yes you DID', 'No I DIDN'T'.

You may want to write it all down for your own sake, of course – and that's OK. The act of writing will help you to get it off your chest and clarify your mind as to what the issues are and where you stand. But never, *never,* NEVER send it. The act of mailing that letter will be a clear declaration of war – and in a war there are no ultimate winners, only losers.

Remember – writing rights no wrongs, so never send your grievances in a letter. (The same applies, if I may say so, to clergy when they are communicating with their musicians.)

Never argue over the phone

When you talk on the phone, you and the other person are each on your own 'territory' – at home or in the office. And when you attack someone on their territory, they have to defend it – and war will again result.

What is more, you cannot see each other's face, so you won't know how the other is responding to what you are saying. You will be shooting in the dark. A word, once spoken, can never be recalled. And you will both know that war has been declared when one of you slams down the receiver.

It's so easy to allow yourself to be trapped into arguing over the phone when an irate parent calls you. You will have been placed in a no-win situation, so get out of it quickly. As soon as you realise what's happening, say very firmly, 'Perhaps it would be helpful if we discussed this face to face. Let me consult my diary. Thanks for calling. Goodbye.' And then immediately seek advice from your minister.

Never argue face to face

Arguing is always a mistake however right you feel you may be, because the essence of an argument is that each of you is saying, 'I'm right and you're wrong.' You may indeed be right, but the other person will never admit that they are wrong, so they will begin to defend themselves, and thus another war will have been declared. Wars never solve anything and people's minds are never changed through arguing: their position is only further strengthened.

Academics enjoy arguing, not to change the other person's mind, but to clarify and sharpen the issues in their own minds. In other words, they too are strengthening their own position through arguing.

3. Arrange a meeting

Ask if you may meet the person with whom you are having difficulty, to talk things over. It's important that you always discuss any problems face to face. This will take courage on your part, but it will prove to be a positive step in the right direction.

Decide beforehand what it is that you want from that meeting. Don't just go ahead determined to get your own way, otherwise you're back to confrontation again. Even if the other person does back down and give you what you want, the cost of your victory will be their defeat. A victory means that there has been a war, and we've already seen that war solves nothing.

So don't go to meet your minister or choir parent thinking that it is they who have the problem, not you; and that they should do something about it – that's tantamount to declaring war again. Instead, let your attitude be: 'I have a problem, and I'd be grateful for your help in trying to solve it.' You will then have to put your problem into words that will not threaten your minister or your choir parent.

Therefore, your ultimate aim should be that both of you, you and your minister, or you and that parent, come out of your meeting feeling good about each other; feeling that you now understand each other's point of view, and you are both willing to meet again, if necessary, to explore even more avenues of mutual co-operation. Being kind is often more important than being right.

Beware of emotion

The problem with musicians and clergy is that we tend to respond more with our hearts than our heads – and emotions are very hard to control. It's the same with parents. If you're a parent you'll know that your child, even if he or she is a pain, must have a good reason for that unacceptable behaviour, and that it's probably the teacher's fault. So beware of mothers whose children are threatened. There is such a thing as the tigress-response syndrome. Nothing will prevent a mother from protecting her child if she thinks her child is being harassed. If you've provoked that situation, get out of the way quickly!

A choir director in Indianapolis noted that according to recent studies, one in four congregations is embroiled in leadership conflicts which are mostly to do with the church's music. The music director needs, therefore, to be skilled in person-to-person relationships and be able to say, when challenged, 'Thank you for saying that. Let me think about it and get back to you.'

After one of our Choral Evensongs in Princeton, when the organ scholar played a demanding piece by Tournemire, a member of the congregation wrote to me to complain about the noisy voluntary. She accused the organist of 'showing off'. I wrote back to her to thank her for writing to me and added that I would discuss the matter fully with the Rector and the organ scholar. I showed the letters to the Rector, but not the organ scholar (because he had been offering his gifts to God) and the Rector approved of my peace-making answer. The complainant was also satisfied, because all she wanted was to know that her complaint had been heard. That is what most people want – to be taken seriously and to be treated courteously.

The best meeting place?

Where should you meet to talk? In your office or your minister's office? In your home or the parent's home?

It's a fifty-fifty situation. If your minister meets you in your office, he or she is coming into your territory by invitation. Therefore you have to show them the courtesy expected of a host; you have to hold back – which might be a good thing.

If you meet in the minister's office, the minister will have to hold back to show you courtesy, but you will feel slightly uncomfortable because you're in his or her home territory.

Start positively

Always, *always*, ALWAYS start your meeting by saying something positive and complimentary to your host. 'I did appreciate your sermon last week – it helped me to think about . . .'; 'What a lovely home you have. What is that picture . . .?' Such an opening will oil the wheels of communication between you, and thus set the mood for what you've come to talk about. You want the other person really to hear what it is that you have to say, and a sincere compliment is the surest way to open their ears. We all like to listen when people say nice things about us.

Be conciliatory

Don't be threatening or confrontational. Don't just wade in bluntly by saying: 'I can't possibly play the sort of music you want me to play,' or 'Your child is being a real nuisance.' Say instead, 'I do want to help the congregation in its worship, especially with the new music which we're using. Is there any way you can help me do this better?'

Or, 'I really enjoy having William in my choir. He's got a lot of energy, hasn't he; but I wonder how I can help him to enjoy our rehearsals more?'

By taking this approach the other person will see, immediately, that you are there in the spirit of peace and conciliation, and so they will tend to answer you in similar terms. Always, *always*, ALWAYS, when there is a danger of confrontation, try to see things from the other person's point of view. 'How would I feel if I were the minister? How would I feel if William were my son?'

(Let me contradict myself for a moment here, and say the exact opposite of what I said earlier about regarding the problem as my problem and not their problem. Sometimes you find that a person will unload a problem onto you. You might have a boss, for instance, who is difficult to get along with and who makes your life very uncomfortable. That can immediately put a burden onto you when in fact that problem doesn't belong to you but to the other person. One of the most helpful lessons I've learnt in life is to realise that when this sort of thing happens it's not *my* problem, but *their* problem. This tends, immediately, to set me free from the load of you-know-what that they've thrown at me.

But you must never tell them that it's their problem. That is for your internal digestion only. 'A difficult person is a person with a difficulty.' You have to feel sorry for them, for they are in their own private prison. This can apply to all walks of life, whether it be a shop assistant who is trying to serve a disagreeable customer, or a choir director who has an unco-operative singer. Don't allow their deep-seated problems to upset you.)

But let's get back to that meeting with your minister or parent –

Prepare yourself

We have already seen the need to be positive in everything you say. But if you're the sort of person who will find this difficult, you'll have to work out in advance of your meeting what you *need* to say (not what you *want* to say).

In fact, even if you are tactful by nature, you would still be wise to prepare what you need to say beforehand. Your meeting will be a turning point in your life and in your minister's or parent's life, and you need to come away from it with both of you feeling positive and eager and willing to co-operate further.

Listen first, speak second

Once you've posed the problem in positive terms, let your minister or parent speak for as long as they like. Do NOT interrupt, however much you may disagree, unless it is to murmur, 'Yes, I agree' or 'I see what you mean'. Sit facing that person, so that your body language says, 'I am giving you my whole attention.' By letting the other person speak without interruption, you are enabling them to get the problem off their chest. If they speak for fifteen minutes, let them. The longer they speak, the less 'ammunition' they will have to fire at you later on (should it come to that) when it's your turn.

When they stop talking, immediately say one or two sentences to show that you really have been listening, such as: 'Thank you for explaining your plans for the music of our church so clearly. I didn't realise . . .'; 'Thank you for telling me some things about William which I didn't know. I found that so helpful.'

And then, follow that up by putting forward your own views, albeit still presented positively: 'May I tell you something of my own musical background, for I need to know more about these new tunes', or 'The children in our choir come from many different backgrounds, and several of them need more help to get on better with the others.'

4. Arrange another meeting

The ultimate aim of the first meeting, should no solution be forthcoming, is to plan another meeting. So make sure that you part like reasonable adults, respecting each other even more than before, because of what each has learnt from the other and because of the positive and helpful way that you have both conducted yourselves.

Again, that will take enormous self-control on your part – especially if the other person begins to lose their cool. A calm answer will turn away wrath, for it takes two to make a fight. If your whole demeanour says, 'I really do respect you and I am positively oozing with goodwill right now,' the other person will have nothing to hit. Take your time before answering – count slowly up to three and breathe deeply. And if you can't think of an answer which will help the situation, say, 'That's a most important point. Let me think about it.'

And so, if after twenty or thirty minutes you find that no course of action has been agreed, bring the meeting to a close by saying, 'Thank you for being so helpful. I wonder if we could meet again soon to discuss this further?'

Then follow that up by sending a short, handwritten note to your minister/parent thanking them for that wholly positive meeting. 'I feel greatly encouraged by what we said to each other, and look forward to our next meeting.' One should never communicate destructive matters in writing (as I said earlier), but one should write as many 'thank you' letters as possible. People love to be thanked, and this oils the wheels of personal relationships and positive communication more than you could imagine. The sooner a letter is received, the more it means. If it is delayed, its effect is much less. So write your letter as soon as you return home. That will sow good seed for your next meeting, which may eventually bring forth ripe fruit which you may both enjoy.

But the very first question I should ask myself when a problem arises between me and my minister, or with another adult, is: How much of this problem is my fault? It takes two to make a quarrel. Therefore, before I try to take the beam from the other's eye, I may need to acknowledge that I do have a speck in my own eye which I need to deal with. This will not be easy, but it will go a long way to prepare for a happier outcome to my problem.

CHAPTER 27

New music

What can you do if your minister wants you to perform music which you don't like – because it's not the sort of music you have been trained to appreciate, and it doesn't always sound right on the organ?

Take a professional approach

Don't fall into the danger of deciding, perhaps unconsciously, not to play it very well. ('I'll show the minister that the congregation can't sing this rubbish!') Your professional expertise should enable you to say, 'I'll do my very best to turn this rubbish into music.'

I've been there, and I know what I'm talking about. It gave me great pride, on one occasion, to turn one awful hymn tune that my minister told me to play into real music. I reharmonised it, wrote a descant and rehearsed the choir so that it sounded really well. It's now become an annual favourite.

If Martin Neary, at Princess Diana's funeral, could accept so-called pop music into the service in Westminster Abbey, none of us has a leg to stand on when we are asked, or told, to do something similar. It worked at the Abbey because it was done superbly. That should also be our aim.

If this new music doesn't fit on the organ, then play it on the piano. If you still can't present it as it should be presented, then have it played by guitars and drums for which it may have been written. There may be some young people in your church who would be pleased to be asked to lead the worship for that new song. That would relieve you of the responsibility for its performance, and let you play on the organ only what sounds well on that instrument.

Adapting to change

We are living in a new age. Discovering how to manage change is one of the most important skills we need to learn. Change is in the air, and if we are to take a creative and constructive part in that change, we have to stay on board. 'The church's one foundation' and music by Stanford still have their place – but other music must be given its chance in today's worship, however much some may not like it. It's all happened before. The exquisitely spiritual music of Byrd over four hundred years ago was replaced by the dancy, theatrical music of Purcell. And yet, today, we love them both. There's nothing new under the sun.

What I'm saying is that there are new ways of doing things, and we must be prepared to give them a fair chance. If you don't bend with the wind, you'll break. The reason why dinosaurs died out millions of years ago while other species survived, is that unlike those species dinosaurs couldn't adapt to the great changes that were taking place on the earth at that time.

I know you can't abide some of this new music and you resent the sound of guitars in church when the organ is the only instrument the Almighty really likes. But do you want to survive and to grow? Do you want, actively, to mold the changes that are coming? Or are you a dinosaur? It's up to you.

If this new music helps some in their quest to find God, then surely we should rejoice with them and help them in their spiritual journey. It was said of the sculptor, Henry Moore, that he could only worship God through his sculptures. Perhaps we can only find God through the music of Palestrina, but that does not mean that such music is the *only* way to God.

On the other hand, we need to bear in mind that, not only is there beauty in holiness, there is also holiness in beauty. Does this proposed new music add beauty to the worship, or is it a sop to the congregation? What is remembered in worship and what can influence lives, is a sense of transcendence, and this may come from the music as much as, or more than, from the preaching. But when you discuss these matters with your minister, you have to approach them very carefully and tactfully – with an open mind and a willing and co-operative spirit. In fact, why don't you take an active part in trying to find some new music which both you and your minister would like? There's a lot of it about and, that way, you would become part of the solution rather than part of the problem.

A last resort – resignation

If you've tried your very best and really 'given it a go', but still find that it doesn't work for you, then it may well be that for the good of your church and your own peace of mind you should consider resignation. Look at the situation as calmly as you can. (I know that's difficult, for you have given your best to that church for a long time and your choir and the congregation have appreciated what you have done for them.) But if you feel that the misunderstandings will not only continue but even get worse, then the time may have come for a graceful exit.

Your vocation was to bring the beauty of harmony to

that church. Let the manner of your leaving add to that harmony. Don't destroy what you have so painstakingly created. That would hurt you even more than it would hurt them. Be kind to yourself, and let love rule your head as well as your heart.

CHAPTER 28

The new choir director

A new broom?

When a new choir director is appointed, changes are bound to take place. But the trouble is that change is nearly always regarded as a threat or a loss. We all like things to stay as they are, even if they aren't always wholly right. Change means going out into the unknown, leaving behind the comfort of the things that are known. Many of us like life to be undemanding, for then we don't have to make any effort. Change means that we have to rethink our position and so have to take a different course of action from the one which seems to have served us well in the past, and with which we were comfortable.

But the good is the enemy of the best. So often we put up with the second best. Some choirs are content to say that they've done it that way ever since dear old so-and-so was choir director, and so why change? The suggestion by a new choir director that there may be a better way to do things makes everyone immediately uneasy.

The new choir director is not only likely to introduce changes, but could be said to have a duty to do so. Change is not only a challenge but also a great opportunity for improvement. But how should those changes be introduced?

Valuing past good

If a young director is taking over from a more experienced conductor who's done a really good job, the new man or woman should first be willing to take on board as many good things as possible from the legacy of their predecessor. Then new ways will be based on a good foundation and will be more readily accepted by the choir.

A pastoral approach

New ways should be introduced in a pastoral manner, to enable as many folk as possible to feel that they might be willing to try them.

To do that you have first to earn the right to be heard. Choir directors should not make major changes which might be controversial until they have been in their new job for at least a year. During that time they can assess the situation carefully, discuss it with the minister and other wise friends and, at the same time, gradually earn the respect of their choir.

You have to show that you are a worthy choir director who can do some things better than your predecessor, so that you may steadily become known and loved by all your singers.

This means spending time with them and getting to know them (and their families) individually, through visiting them in their homes. It means showing yourself to be a friendly person both on and off duty, and loving them by being able to listen to what they say to you, and responding in a thoughtful and attentive manner. It means writing 'thank you' notes to them after major musical events, remembering their birthdays, and praying for them and sending them get-well cards when they, or members of their families, are sick. It means inviting them to your home. A choral director is, as I've said before, a pastor to his or her flock.

Introduce change gradually

One effective, non-threatening way to introduce change is to say, 'Let's try this for a clearly defined short time, to see if it works.' For example, trying out a different seating plan for the choir, or experimenting with a different time to begin your rehearsals. Most folk would be willing to go along with that if they see that they will have a vote as to whether or not it should continue. And everyone will feel easier about trying it if they know it is only, say, for a month.

If the experiment doesn't work, then, quite clearly, you should return to what you did before – for the old way will have proved itself to be the better way. If, on the other hand, the new way does seem to be more suitable, then you could suggest that the trial period could be extended, after which everyone can have their say again. Once that stage has been accepted, it's more likely that the change will become permanent.

Someone is almost certain not to agree to the change, and, since life is not perfect, compromise needs always to be considered – as long as you don't allow that person, whoever it may be, to overrule everyone else's opinions.

Don't make changes too soon

Let me underline this point once more: if you are starting a new job, don't introduce too many changes too soon. You have to work your way into the situation to discover what does and doesn't work. I know of several talented choir directors who started new jobs and made sweeping changes before they had been in their post for more than a few days.

One choir director, who took over a run-down choir, found that there was a built-in resistance to the changes he wanted to introduce and, in the end, he had to leave when he'd been there for less than a year. Another choir director inherited a thriving choir programme, but he also made sweeping changes without experiencing why that programme had been so successful, and this upset a lot of dedicated people needlessly.

Summing up

Introduce changes slowly, after lots of consultation, so that you may carry the majority of your singers, and the parish, with you. That way everyone will be a winner. Appreciate what was good about your predecessor's programme, and build on that sure foundation.

I'm happy to confess that I have learned more from assimilating what my predecessors had achieved in the three major musical posts I held during my professional career than from almost any other source. We can all learn from our predecessors and incorporate their achievements into our own musical skills, not only for the benefit of those we serve, but also so that we ourselves may continue to grow. When we stop learning we stop living.

There's a well-known prayer by Reinhold Niebuhr* which sums this up nicely:

> O God, grant us
> the serenity to accept what cannot be changed,
> the courage to change what can be changed,
> and the wisdom to know the difference.

* From *Justice and Mercy*, edited by Ursula Niebhur, published by Harper and Row.

CHAPTER 29

The Christian element

Communicating faith

If you're conducting a choir in a Christian church you will have many opportunities to share your faith with your singers and their families, even though this is not always easy to do.

It is important that you show that what we are singing about has to do with ultimate, practical reality – we're not singing about half truths, but eternal truths, and these truths have molded countless lives for well over 2000 years.

It has been said that we can't communicate Christ to others until we have discovered him for ourselves. We can only pass on to others what we ourselves have received. If we have a passion for choir training, we will almost automatically pass that enthusiasm on to our choir. If we have a lively faith in a living Lord, that too will be communicated to our choir – sometimes without our being aware of it. If, on the other hand, our faith is a theoretical faith gleaned from books and not from our own daily experience, then that also will be passed on to those who are nearest to us. It will be a theoretical faith, and theory is, by definition, boring – until it is made immediately practical.*

If you were to ask me whether I think that directors of Christian choirs need to have a lively faith, I would have to answer, 'Yes'. I was told, when I led my choir programme in America, that choir directors have more Christian influence over the children in their choirs than the minister. This is because the choir director sees them more frequently and interacts with them more closely than the minister. And so the effect that this can have on the lives of one's choristers, be they children or adults, is awesome.

It was my privilege, when at Trinity Church, Princeton, to lead the choirboys' confirmation class each week after morning service. I cannot tell you how much that meant to me. I found that, instead of sharing my faith with them, they often shared their faith with me. It was a tremendously strengthening time for us all, and I received a lot of positive feed-back from their parents.

* For help in this direction see www.alphacourse.org.uk and for the *Emmaus* teaching programme see www.eri.org/

The importance of prayer

The essence of the Christian life, surely, is an inter-active relationship with a living, loving God, i.e. not praying to a brick wall, but praying to the God who invented listening and therefore hears your prayer. We then, having prayed, need to look actively for an answer to our prayer. That's the only way to find out what the answer will be.

1. Praying with the choir

Many church choirs begin their rehearsals with a prayer. If you don't feel able to do this yourself, talk it over with your minister and find, perhaps, an adult singer who would like to lead the prayers for you. In some churches there may be more than one adult who would like to do this, and so they could take it in turns. Sometimes the singers like to join in the prayer themselves, and this can be very meaningful for them.

Here are some prayer suggestions:

The Choristers' Prayer
Bless, O Lord, us thy servants, who minister in thy temple;
    grant that what we sing with our lips,
    we may believe in our hearts,
    and what we believe in our hearts,
    we may show forth in our lives;
    through Jesus Christ our Lord. Amen.

A prayer for Church Musicians
O God, whom saints and angels delight to worship in heaven:
    be ever present with your servants,
    who seek through art and music to perfect the praises
    offered by your people on earth;
    and grant to them even now glimpses of your beauty,
    and make them worthy at length
    to behold it unveiled for ever more;
    through Jesus Christ our Lord. Amen.

At the end of the rehearsal, you and your singers could pray:

Remember, O Lord, what thou hast wrought in us,
    and not what we deserve;
    and as thou hast called us to thy service,
    make us worthy of our calling.

The Grace could follow this prayer, or be used on its own.

Some choirs have more elaborate prayers. When I guest conducted the choir of the Crystal Cathedral in Garden Grove, California, they were very well organised indeed.

Two members of the eighty-strong adult choir had been appointed as lay chaplains. One led the prayers for the Thursday night rehearsal, and the other on Sunday morning.

They each chose a short passage to read from the Bible, and gave a very brief commentary. Then we prayed for those in the choir and their families who needed prayer. This only lasted five minutes, but it was a wonderful way to start a rehearsal because it gave us all a feeling of unity and emphasised for us all why we were there. I commend it to you.

2. Praying for the choir

A choir director friend in southern California gave me another idea which we adopted in Princeton. Every young singer in our choirs, from the smallest child to the most senior high-school pupil, had a specific member of the congregation who had undertaken to pray for him or her. We called this our Prayer Partner Programme, which made an appropriate quasi-acronym for our singers – PPP.

It took a lot of organising, but we had a choir parent who was very good at organisation. She kept a record of all the children who sang in our choirs, for we had children joining us not only at the beginning of the season, but throughout the year. And, of course, we had some children leaving us when their parents moved away.

It was the same with people who wanted to become prayer partners. There were many folk who volunteered for this and followed up faithfully, and there were some who were well-intentioned but didn't follow up.

(By the way, there are some proven statistics regarding volunteers. When you ask for volunteers to do anything, 25 per cent will help you wholeheartedly, 50 per cent will join in quite well, but the remaining 25 per cent won't turn up at all. It's just as well to know that when you ask for volunteers, so that you aren't too disappointed when you aren't given support as fully as you expected.)

Our Prayer Partner co-ordinator arranged for members of the congregation and adults in the choirs to sign up as prayer partners – one per child. She then compiled a card with the singer's photograph, plus information about home, family and school life. She discovered from the child's parents what to pray for and then she gave the card to the prayer partner.

I told the children that this new programme was beginning, and that every child should be aware that they were being prayed for. Parents and children were encouraged to contact the co-ordinator so that she could pass along prayer needs or praise reports to the prayer partner.

In order to keep the contact alive during the season, cards were sent several times a year to the parents of the children and also to the partners. This kept them in touch and encouraged them to make the best use of the programme.

We asked the prayer partners to pray for their singers every day, and to send their 'choir children' cards on their birthdays and at Christmas. We asked them to know their singers well enough to be able to greet them by name when they saw them on Sundays or bumped into them on the street. We didn't ask for more than this, for it could have become too burdensome, both for the prayer partners and also for the children. The organiser, on her part, sent to each prayer partner news of his or her child's progress, or other news, so that the lines of communication remained open.

At the end of the season we ensured that each child wrote a 'thank you' note to his or her prayer partner. That brought a sense of closure to the year, and it enabled partners to withdraw from the scheme if they wanted to.

The scheme was a way for people to share their Christian faith with the young singers and offer them support. We also found that some of the adult singers were being prayed for regularly by members of the congregation, and that really helped to bring the whole church even more closely together.

In addition, it is helpful if you, as the choir director, pray regularly for the members of your choir by name. That, at the very least, sows seeds of love to your singers, which must bring forth good fruit. And, of course, you should pray for your minister too, because your minister is almost certainly praying for you.

Pastoral playing for weddings and funerals

It's so easy for us organists to regard the playing for weddings and funerals as little more than a means of earning extra fees. It's only when one of our friends or relations is married or buried that we realise, all too briefly, what a very important service it is and how much the music means to those present.

What a privilege it is to be a church musician – but how much more of a privilege and responsibility it is to make music for those who are starting their lives together, and for those who have finished their course. May we ever play not only with our heads but also with our hearts.

CHAPTER 30

Finding sufficient energy to lead a rehearsal at the end of a busy day

Tired out

At the end of a day's hard work you may feel that you don't have enough energy to lead your choir practice. But don't tell your choir that you're feeling tired. Deal with your tiredness more positively than that.

Try taking a five minute rest before you go out for your rehearsal. You may think you can't do that because you don't have time – what with the demands of your family, and all sorts of other things you have to do. But if one of your children cut her finger or had a problem with her homework, you'd give *her* five minutes of your time – so surely you can find five minutes to prepare yourself physically and mentally for your choir practice. It's a matter of priorities.

All you need is five minutes to lie flat on the floor of your bedroom, relaxing with deep breathing, so that your singers who are waiting for you will, like your family, receive the best from your personal attention.

You see, being a choral director is very similar to being an actor. When you enter your practice room, you are 'on stage'; you have to put on a 'good show' for the benefit of all those who will gain from what you are about to give them. Even if you feel tired or ill, you are not allowed to unload your problems onto your singers, for it is they who should feel free to unload their problems onto you.

It's all a question of will-power. I'm not a 'morning' person, and so, on Sunday mornings when I was about to enter the practice room of my church in the USA, I consciously used to take a couple of deep breaths when I got out of my car, and then I bounced into the room and said a cheerful 'Good morning' to the singers as they arrived. I made myself do it – and, do you know, after a couple of minutes I actually began to feel cheerful and awake and ready to start. This was because my singers responded to my ebullient 'on stage' mood, and their enthusiasm began to feed me.

On the other hand, I knew one choir director who quite clearly unloaded his problems onto his choir on a regular basis. He often had had a busy day, and his bad moods permeated his whole choir. I don't know why they put up with him.

By the way, be aware that the weather can influence your mood and the mood of your choir. If the atmosphere is close and stormy you may all feel a little unsettled; and when it's spring, you may all feel chirpy! Adolescents tend to become particularly lively in the springtime. Point this out to them so that they can, the more readily, control their natural inclinations.

Irene Willis

The person who gave me an example which I have ever before me is my first associate director at Trinity Church, Princeton – Irene Willis. She had boundless energy, superb leadership skills and overflowing love to all with whom she worked. She was a human dynamo.

It would be easy to assume that she had no problems in her life. But, oh yes she did! She shared some of them with me during our weekly one-on-one staff meetings. Horrendous things were happening to her, but when she led the adult choir practice the same evening, nobody would have guessed what she was going through. She was ever cheerful, ever ebullient and ever full of energy.

Then she was appointed director of music of St James's Church, Madison Avenue, New York – which is one of the leading churches in that city. One month after she began there she phoned me to say that she had cancer of the lungs and that she would, therefore, be dead within a year. We prayed and wept together on the phone, and then she began a painful course of chemotherapy. That was in September.

On Christmas Eve she was so ill that she couldn't talk, and yet she went to her church to lead the choir rehearsal for the midnight service. She wrote on the blackboard, 'I can't talk, so I'll write what I want you to do.'

And so, when I think that I'm not feeling quite up to the mark to lead my choir rehearsals, I think of Irene, and I gird my loins and make myself go and do it, for that is why I was appointed.

Feeling better

Sometimes, you will feel better after a demanding rehearsal than you did before it started. Recent research with some choirs in California* has shown that a protein used by the immune system to fight disease increased by 150 per cent during choir rehearsals and by 240 per cent during concerts. Singing not only made the singers healthier, but it also made them feel happier. The same can be true for your choir if you lead your rehearsals positively

* Marla Jo Fisher. Copyright 2001: The Orange County Register.

and cheerfully and productively – this healthier state of mind and body will in turn affect you.

When you take seriously your vocation as a choral director, you will not allow your own feelings of lassitude, illness or whatever to come between you and your singers. They are there to be inspired by you, so, inspire them. You have to create a mood of expectancy in your choir from the first minute of your rehearsal – or even before the practice begins – by your interacting with your singers informally when they arrive. Once you have begun to inspire your singers, they, in their turn, will begin to inspire you and so, at the end of the rehearsal, both you and they will know that you have, between you, created something thoroughly worthwhile, and you will all go home tired but also happier and healthier.

CHAPTER 31

A lesson in dedication – Sir David Willcocks

Let me tell you a true story. When I was a student at Cambridge, no outsider was ever allowed to observe the choir of King's College rehearsing in the chapel. For example, my teacher, Boris Ord, who directed the choir at that time, was rehearsing them in the chapel one day when the Provost of King's (the President of the College) walked in with the Duke of Edinburgh, who was later to become Chancellor of the University. Dr Ord, hearing them enter, half turned to see who it was, turned back to his choir and said, 'Thank you, gentlemen, that will be all!' – and the choir walked out. Such was the strength of that prohibition.

This discipline was also strong under Boris Ord's successor, David Willcocks. But I wrote to him to say that I would be coming to Cambridge for a few days and asked if he would allow me to watch him rehearse his choir in the chapel. He'd been at Cambridge for about ten years and I was a cathedral organist and had known him for all that time. He wrote me a kind letter saying that he looked forward to seeing me again, and telling me to wait outside the chapel and he would let me in to observe his rehearsal.

I got to the chapel very early and waited outside, because the gates were locked. Fifteen minutes before the practice was due to begin the sixteen trebles appeared, wearing their top hats and gowns. The sexton unlocked the gates and they went in, and I was alone again. Five minutes later the undergraduate choirmen arrived in small groups, wearing their gowns. The sexton again unlocked the gates and they disappeared inside.

Five minutes later I saw David Willcocks coming down the path towards the chapel. He wore a dark suit and his flowing gown, and he carried some music under his arm. He looked every inch a headmaster. I expected him to say, 'Hello, John, how nice to see you. Come along in!' But he didn't. He looked at me for fully three long seconds and said, 'I don't usually do this.' I didn't know what to say to that; but then he went on, 'And so I'd like you to sit as far from the choir as possible without being seen, and please don't make a sound!' I felt like a 6-year-old boy.

I did as I was told and followed him meekly into the silent chapel, found a seat where I could just see the choir without being seen, and for the next hour I watched a most amazing choir practice. But it wasn't what I learned from that choir practice that I remember most vividly. It was what I learned from that traumatic encounter with David Willcocks outside the chapel. That moment was for ever seared upon my consciousness.

Sir David, as he was later to become, had been director of King's choir for many years; he led two choir practices every day – one with the boys first thing in the morning, and another with the full choir every afternoon. There were choral services almost every day. There were broadcasts and recordings and concert tours and television and I don't know what else. But on this particular day there was just a normal rehearsal followed by a service, and Sir David wasn't going to allow that rehearsal to be interrupted by *anyone*, because it was so important to him.

And that's what I learned from that memorable incident. When I lead a practice, if it isn't the most important and the most special hour in my life, then why on earth should my singers regard it as important and special to them? If I'm not prepared to give my very, very best to my singers, some of whom may have travelled quite long distances to be at my rehearsal, why on earth should they give their best to me?

I confess that I sometimes forget this lesson. There was an occasion a few years ago, when I was leading a probationers' practice at my church in Princeton – with half a dozen 8-year-old girls. They were singing badly, they were out of tune, they weren't concentrating and they were making a nasty noise. It was raining outside and everyone felt damp, cold and miserable. The thought came to me, 'I've got college degrees; why on earth am I wasting my time with these unresponsive little girls?' And then I remembered David Willcocks, and it was almost as though a voice came to me from heaven, saying, 'This is exactly why I've brought you here – so get on with it!' And so I sat up straight and began to give those girls my fullest attention. I gave them my very, very best; and do you know, they suddenly started to sing beautifully for me. I was thrilled.

Sir David has given me permission to tell this story, so that it may help others as much as it has helped me. None of us who are called to be leaders dares to give anything less than our very, very best at all times, and the rewards exceed anything that we could ever imagine.

CHAPTER 32

Five key words

These five words, beginning with the same letter, can help to transform your approach to your choir and so improve their singing immediately.

1. Lead

The choral director must give a firm, unequivocal lead in everything he or she does. If you don't lead your choir, your choir will lead you. They will lead you into accepting unpunctuality, accepting wrong notes, putting up with inattention and accepting all those other faults which so many choirs share, because their directors don't lead – they follow.

Robert Boughen, organist of Brisbane Cathedral, gave a lecture at a choir course I was directing in Perth, Australia, some years ago, in which he said that the secret of good choir organisation was to have some. I've always remembered that sentence because it means that, when things go wrong in your choir, it's almost certainly because you, their director, haven't done anything to put them right. Think about it!

And so you must lead your choir firmly, cheerfully and confidently in all things that are good – through doing your homework so that you will know exactly what to rehearse and how to rehearse it – always being cheerful (especially when you don't feel cheerful), always giving out energy (especially when you are tired), always giving directions clearly and precisely with lively eye contact, and always encouraging your singers to do even better this week than they did last week. Thus your authority will grow.

Train your choir – by giving the responsibility to them – to lead the congregation in its singing, its saying and its understanding. Train them to show the congregation, through self-disciplined example, how to worship.

When you find yourself 'putting up' with an unsatisfactory situation in your choir, could it be because you are not leading them with sufficient firmness? Nettles are meant to be grasped.

2. Learn

Always be learning how to do your job better. Once you stop learning you stop living. The best leaders are always seeking ways to improve their leadership. When things go wrong in rehearsals (as they will) learn from your mistakes and put them right next week.

Your singers need to learn something specific from you each week. That's easy when you have a children's choir, for you will have a clearly defined structure of learning set out for them. (You do, don't you?) But adults also need to learn something from you each week. For instance, let there be a steady programme of teaching sight-singing by spending at least two one-minute periods in each rehearsal when you demonstrate why a dotted note is worth one and a half undotted notes, or why the second line up on the treble stave is a G. If your singers haven't learned anything from you at tonight's rehearsal, you've wasted their time, and yours.

Have you attended courses for choir directors and singers? You can learn so much from them – including what *not* to do. Take some of your singers along with you to enjoy the experience of singing with other musicians. They will come back to your choir enthused to sing even better for you. (See the Appendix for contact addresses.)

3. Look

Look your singers straight in the face when you are talking to them and when you are conducting them. Far too many choral directors don't do this. They look at the music when they give instructions, or they drop their eyes because they lack a real sense of leadership. Officers in the army know that when they are giving an order they must look their soldiers straight in the face. You are the officer; your choir are the troops. Look at them.

And your singers must look at you when you are conducting them. Many of them won't, and so you will have to rehearse them in this: 'Sing that first chord/line from memory, looking at me.' The practice of looking needs to be practised.

When you look at your singers, and your singers look at you, you will experience a sense of unity which will be wonderfully and excitingly creative. You will hold them in the palm of your hands, and you'll be able to mold their singing as though you were a pianist playing a piano. As the keys are responsive to the pianist's hands, so your singers will be responsive to your every direction. Once you and they have experienced this, you will all have reached a new level of achievement.

Also, when there is an instrumental introduction to an anthem, look at your singers with growing intensity during the whole of that introduction, so that they can feel the rising excitement of coming in really together, fully in the spirit of the music. The choir needs to be able to feel why the composer wrote the introduction, and they need to feel those opening bars in their innermost beings – and it's up to you to enable them to do this by the way that you look at them before they sing. The classic example, of course, is Handel's *Zadok the Priest*. There's a full page of introduction to this anthem – which has been called the finest anthem ever written. If you can conduct this so as to enable and inspire your singers eventually to burst in with those triumphant words in such a way that their socks are blown off, you will know what I mean.

Some conductors conduct the organ or orchestra for introductions, and only look at their choir a bar or so before they come in. But every professional singer knows that a great deal of singing is to do with *anticipation*. So, enable your singers to anticipate, to be fully prepared, mentally as well as vocally, to come in with creative musical energy – be the music loud or soft.

Encourage your singers to look at their music intelligently by asking them questions which require them to do so. Thus they will gradually acquire sight-singing skills which will make your task of teaching music so much easier. Many singers can't read music because they only look at the words and listen to the piano or the singer next to them to enable them to sing the right notes. You need to ask specific questions – not saying, 'Look at the music' but, 'Is that first note an F or a G?'; 'Is it a one-beat note or a two-beat note?' (and explain why); 'Should this passage be sung loudly or softly'; 'What does that expression mark mean?'

Once your singers have begun to look at their music intelligently they will begin to experience a new dimension of interest in their membership of your choir.

4. Listen

Listen to your choir when they are singing. Do you hear what they are really doing or do you hear only what you want to hear? Have you grown so used to the tenors singing flat, to the altos singing wrong notes, or the sopranos not blending, that you can no longer hear these shortcomings? Listen to your choir with fresh ears – make a recording of them and take it home to listen to it. You may be surprised what you hear.

Does your choir really listen to you, or do they just hear the noises you make? Do they listen to the chord you give for the unaccompanied anthem (because you play it once), or do they just hear it (because you play it more than once) and so sing not very well in tune?

Do they listen to you when you give instructions – because your instructions are worth listening to and because you give them once? Or do they turn off because you talk too much, and because what you say is not worth listening to? Do you speak with authority?

Do your singers listen to each other, so that they blend and balance and make a lovely sound? Is each singer aware of the singers around them? Can they hear the other singers, or are there so many sopranos bunched together that they can't hear the other voices? In that case you might want to think of rearranging the seating of your singers for an experimental period to see if it improves things – dividing the sopranos so that the other voices can hear them, and they can hear the other voices.

Or do your singers sing out forwards without any regard for the singers around them? If so, you have an assorted group of individual singers and not a choir.

Do you listen to the sounds your organ produces when you play it, or are you only concerned with playing the right notes, and not thinking about what the music means? You know what the organ sounds like at the console, but what is its effect in the church?

Do you listen, really listen, when people talk to you? To give someone your total attention when they want to talk with you is one of the greatest gifts you can give them.

5. Love

Do you love all your singers? Or, if you prefer another word, do you hold each singer in courteous, affectionate respect? Does your love include the ones you find it especially hard to love – the awkward adults and the difficult children. If not, they will know, and they will be unable to give you their best. Love is the oil which enables the machinery of communication to run smoothly.

When you are directing a choir it's essential that you cultivate good personal relationships and good working relationships with all your singers, individually and collectively – be they adults or children.

If you have a 'difficult' choir, you are like a pianist who is trying to play a piano with a faulty mechanism. You may want to play the right notes, but until you've dealt with the unreliable keys you can't do anything but give a bad performance. The piano can't do anything to correct itself; it is the pianist who must take the initiative by looking carefully at the mechanism to discover which particular keys aren't working properly – and put them right. The difference is that a choir has feelings, and a piano doesn't. Therefore you will realise afresh that a significant part of your vocation as a choral director is your skill in handling personal relationships.

Your choir will know instinctively (a) whether or not you like and respect them, both individually and collectively, and (b) whether or not you expect them to excel.

I know this, not only from my own experience, but also from what I read in a book by Barbara Woodhouse, the animal trainer. She said that when a horse is taking part in show jumping, it can tell whether or not its rider really believes that it will jump the next fence successfully. If the rider feels, 'I don't think we're going to make it this time', the horse somehow will get that message and fail.

It's the same with a choir. They will know what you feel about them, however hard you try to cover up your feelings. If you feel, 'I'm tired tonight, and so we won't have a good practice', your feelings will come true. If you feel, 'I don't like some of these singers – I wish they weren't here', your singers will know, and so they won't co-operate.

Therefore, you should go to your practice room with your mind geared up to radiate joyful, loving expectancy at the prospect of all the good things you're going to achieve together tonight. I confess that that's exactly what I do myself. I consciously create in my mind an attitude of love and co-operation and expectancy towards all my singers, so that I know we're going to have a great practice. (And, of course, I've also done my homework.) That's why my singers enjoy my rehearsals and why they achieve so much.

What you feel about your singers, they will quickly feel about you. You are the leader in all things. Your choir must have high expectations of you and you must have high expectations of them. And it's you who must set that mood even before the rehearsal begins, by interacting with your singers as they arrive.

If you have a difficult person in your choir – someone with an attitude problem – it's up to you to charm, to encourage and inspire that person to become co-operative because you are the leader. If you feel that person is dominating you, then that person becomes the leader. But no, *you* are the leader, so cast away your feelings of dislike (which are basically rooted in fear) and actively begin to treat that person as a friend. Deep down they must have some measure of goodwill towards the choir, otherwise they wouldn't be there – so start working on that seed of goodwill and feed and water it patiently. It will eventually bear fruit.

So it all comes back to you. You are the leader – and a difficult situation calls for action, not complaining. If the situation seems impossible you may need to call in outside help – a conductor who knows more about choirs and who would be pleased to direct a special rehearsal. Your choir would enjoy being led for such a rehearsal by a guest conductor. Make it an even more special occasion by inviting families, friends and other choir directors and singers to come and watch. You could charge them for the privilege, to offset the conductor's fee and also to provide light refreshments afterwards.

Remember that difficult people are nearly always people with a difficulty. Discover what that difficulty is and you'll go a long way to healing the damage which makes that person behave in an unhelpful manner. You'll remember what I said at the very beginning of this book: discuss your major problems with your minister or chairperson. That's one reason why they're there – to help you do your job to the very best of your ability.

If you do not love your singers, especially the difficult ones – those who come late, those who talk, and those whose voices you would rather not have in your choir – you are not fulfilling your vocation as a leader; your singers will not learn from you, they will not look up to you, they will not listen to you and they will certainly not love or respect you. So the whole choir will suffer.

It is you who must give the lead in the matter of loving. If you have a problem singer, sit down in a chair before your practice and will yourself to love that singer during tonight's rehearsal. You may be surprised that they will sing much better for you, and you might find that you are beginning to like them. Once you know why they behave as they do, you will the more easily begin to understand them. To know all is to forgive all.

And you must love the music you ask your choir to sing. If you don't really care for it, your choir will quickly sense your lack of commitment (however much you may think you've hidden it) and they will not try so hard. One of the essential criteria for leading a well-disciplined choir is to have a love, a passion, for all the music you teach them. Thus they too will share that love and give you their wholehearted commitment.

Every creative process involves pain and hard work. And so when you experience pain, know that this is part of the job. When you find that the going is hard, know that this is also part of the job. But know too that after the pain will come joy – joy for you and joy for your choir, and joy for those who listen to your choir.

Love is the strongest power there is (see 1 Corinthians 13). St Paul was right.

CHAPTER 33
This is what it's all about

A personal experience

A few years ago I was in South Africa just before apartheid was lifted, and during my four week tour I spent two days in East London where I conducted a massed choirs' festival. The next afternoon I was due to fly elsewhere to lead some more workshops in that great country, and so I had the morning free.

My hostess asked if I would be prepared to spend an hour listening to a junior school choir of deprived black children. I agreed. She told me that this choir came from a village where everyone lived in mud huts, and where they had virtually no modern amenities. We couldn't go to them, for it would be dangerous to enter their village, but they could come to us. She warned me that some of the boys sang bass and I had a vision of having to pat little boys on the head as they sang bass to me. And so I girded my loins, mentally, and put on a brave face for the encounter.

Unfortunately there was a misunderstanding as to where we should go to hear this choir, but eventually we discovered that they were waiting for us in the church hall where I'd conducted the festival the day before. We rushed over there and entered the hall ten minutes late.

I shall never forget what I saw. When my hostess and I entered the hall we saw forty children between the ages of fourteen and eighteen, immaculately dressed in green blazers and gray pants or skirts, standing absolutely still on three risers on the stage with their shoulders interlocked, ready to sing. And they were all waiting, silently, for me.

Their school was so deprived that the standard of education they received was only up to junior school grade, and that was all the formal education they could expect. I didn't know that at the time, but my hostess told me afterwards that, in order to get a good job, those black children would need a high school diploma, and there was no way that most of them would ever get that far. Their outlook, therefore, was very bleak.

But the one thing they did have was to belong to the finest choir I have ever heard. As soon as they opened their mouths to sing, I knew they were something very special indeed. Everything was unaccompanied. Their first song began in unison and I was captivated by the glorious sounds they made as they sang, keeping their eyes riveted onto the diminutive woman who conducted them. And then they suddenly burst into four-part harmony, and I was swept away by their singing. They clearly adored their conductor – you could see it in their faces – and she equally clearly loved all of them.

I stood in the centre of the hall so that I could see them all and so that they could all see me, for they had come from their village several miles away solely to sing to me. I cannot tell you the effect that that had on me. I had never experienced anything like it.

After they had finished their first song I went up to thank them and to tell them that I'd never heard a choir sing so marvellously, but my eyes filled with tears and I was not very coherent.

I didn't know what would happen next, until their conductor came up to me and said, 'We'd like to sing some more songs to you.' And so I went back to my place in the centre of the hall and stood there for the next fifty-five minutes, absolutely transfixed as they continued singing to me. Sometimes the girls sang on their own, most beautifully, and sometimes it was the boys, equally sensitively. Sometimes it was a smaller group of mixed voices, and at other times it was the full choir, but their was no break in the discipline as some singers left the stage and others came on. They processed in groups, rhythmically, when leaving the stage to sit in the hall, and they processed back to the stage in the same way, even singing 'getting on stage' songs. I'd never seen anything like it.

There was an infectious vigour and rhythm, and urgency and commitment and pride and self-discipline about their singing which I found hypnotising. Their entire programme was a continuous revelation of what one would normally expect from professional singers led by the finest conductors, and yet, here they were, forty deprived, under-educated black children singing their hearts out exquisitely. And it was all for me.

They sang in several African languages; I had no idea what the songs were called, but one thing I did know was that those children were singing to me about themselves. They were singing about the pride they felt in their long heritage in that most beautiful country. They were singing about times of oppression and hardship. They were singing about the triumph of the spirit in times of great adversity and they believed every word they sang, for they had experienced it at first hand and they knew it to be true.

And after it was all over they remained standing

absolutely still on the stage in three immaculate rows and they looked at me. I asked my hostess if it would be all right if I were to shake them individually by the hand, and she said, 'Yes.' And so I went up to them once more to thank them for giving me an hour which I shall never forget. But as soon as I opened my mouth my eyes began to water, and I couldn't say anything except a very hesitant 'Thank you', as the tears streamed down my face; and I started to go down the front row, looking each singer in the face, giving them all the African double handshake, which they returned firmly as they began to leave.

As I was shaking hands with the singers in the second row, one of the singers in the back row suddenly bent forward and kissed me full on the mouth. I was overwhelmed and stumbled my way through the rest of the singers shaking their hands until they had all left, leaving my hostess and me in that hall all alone.

And so my conception of what can be achieved by choirs was for ever changed that day. Even though I have sometimes been lifted to the very gates of heaven itself by the sublime singing of some world-famous choirs, the choir that I now hold as my ideal – the choir that I try to get my choirs to imitate, alas so inadequately – is that choir of deprived black junior school children who were raised in mud huts in a village where no white person dared to walk.

And they are my ideal not only because they sang with such superb tone and blend and balance and intonation, and stood and processed so impeccably and were dressed in clothes that would have brought credit to the finest school choir anywhere, and not only because they never took their eyes from their conductor for a second – but I hold that choir as my ideal, primarily and unquestionably because they believed with their whole hearts every word that they sang.

And so, I ask myself, 'Do the singers in our own choirs believe every word that they sing?', for that is the most precious blessing we can bestow upon them – the gift of understanding the Gospel and taking it into their hearts. And if they don't yet believe, to whom can they turn for instruction and enlightenment and inspiration except to us, their choral directors?

> Christ has no hands but your hands to do his work this day;
> no other feet but your feet to guide folk on his way;
> no other lips but your lips to tell them why he died;
> no other love but your love to win them to his side.*

* St Teresa of Avila (1515-1582) trans. Evelyn Underhill. *Immanence – a Book of Verses.* J. M. Dent 1913.

APPENDIX

Useful
addresses

American Choral Directors Association (ACDA)
PO Box 6310
Lawton OK 73506, USA

American Guild of Organists (AGO)
475 Riverside Drive, Suite 1260
New York NY 10115, USA
Tel: (001) 212-870-2310
Fax: (001) 212-870-2163
E-mail: info@agohq.org

Association of Anglican Musicians (AAM)
28 Ashton Road
Fort Mitchell KY 41017, USA
Tel/Fax: (001) 606-344-9308
E-mail: AnglicanM@aol.com

Association of British Choral Directors (ABCD)
46 Albert Street
Tring, Herts HP23 6AU
E-mail: marie.louise.petit@abcd.org.uk

Chorus America
2111 Sansom Street
Philadelphia PA 19103, USA

Royal Canadian College of Organists (RCCO)
112 St Clair Avenue West, Suite 302
Toronto, Ontario M4V 2Y3, Canada

Royal College of Organists (RCO)
7 St Andrew Street, London EC4A 3LQ*
Tel: 0207-936-3606
Fax: 0207-353-8244
E-mail: rco@rco.org.uk

Royal School of Church Music (RSCM)
Cleveland Lodge, West Humble
Dorking, Surrey RH5 6BW
Tel: 01306-877676

* The RCO will move to Birmingham in 2004, but their E-mail address will
remain the same.

Fax: 01306-887260
Music supplies fax: 01306-887240
E-mail: musicsupplies@rscm.com
Website: www.rscm.org *(for details of music for choirs of all kinds and practical assistance for your church and school music programme)*
'Voice for Life' - a graduated training programme for choristers
E-mail: voiceforlife@rscm.com

Royal School of Church Music in America (RSCM/A)
1361 West Market Street
Akron OH 44313, USA
Tel: (001) 330-836-1511
Fax: (001) 330-836-1012
Website: www.rscmamerica.org *(for details of annual courses in USA for choir singers and choir directors)*

Trinity College (International centre for music examinations)
89 Albert Embankment
London SE1 7TP
Tel: 0207-820-6100
Fax: 0207-820-6161

The Incorporated Society of Musicians
Tel: 0207-629-4413
Fax: 0207-408-1538
E-mail: membership@ism.org
(The ISM is the UK's professional body for musicians which can give advice on fees and legal matters, as well as comprehensive back-up for every aspect of the music profession.)

Church Music page: www.anonymous@threadnet.com

British Federation of Music Festivals
198 Park Lane
Macclesfield, Cheshire SK11 6UD
Tel: 01625-428-297
Fax: 01625-503-229
Website: www.FESTIVALS@compuserve.com

Dr John Bertalot
E-mail: john@bertalot.demon.co.uk
Website: http://www.metanoia.org/johnbertalot

John Bertalot's first two best-selling books on choirtraining

FIVE WHEELS TO SUCCESSFUL SIGHT-SINGING

'If you buy only one book this year, this should be it.'

Dr Austin Lovelace, Choristers Guild, USA

IMMEDIATELY PRACTICAL TIPS FOR CHORAL DIRECTORS

'If you have time to read only one book... read this.'

Gordon Appleton,
Regional Director, RSCM, England